Lessons from the Zoo

TEN ANIMALS THAT
CHANGED MY LIFE

J. D. Porter

Copyright © 2020 by J. D. Porter

All rights reserved. No part of this publication may be reproduced, distributed or transmitted in any form or by any means, including photocopying, recording, or other electronic or mechanical methods, without the prior written permission of the author, except in the case of brief quotations embodied in critical reviews and certain other noncommercial uses permitted by copyright law.

Lessons from the Zoo/ J. D. Porter. —1st ed.

ISBN 978-1-7353155-2-2

Contents

Introduction 1
Showdown with an Elephant 9
Close Call with a Big Cat 29
A Trailblazing Mule 43
Do unto Apes 63
A Fear of Snakes 77
Never Too Old to Learn 89
Adapting to Change 101
A Failure to Communicate 111
An Appreciation of Nature 123
Seize the Day 135
Love Your Neighbor 145

To the Zookeepers.

We dealt with icy, treacherous winter roads; isolated, lonely locations; and challenging animal medical conditions. We were kicked, bitten, and head-butted, and at the end of the day, we gathered at the Glen Eagles Pub to laugh at our tribulations.

Introduction

"What's your favorite animal?"

That is the second question I get from people who have just asked me what I do for a living. I have been trying to answer it for nearly fifty years—first as a zookeeper, then as a zoo curator, and now as a retired zoo director. I have always answered it in the moment, which means the answer has not always been the same. I have, at times, said the elephant was my favorite animal because of some unique experiences I had with them early in my career. I answered hoofed stock when I remembered the astonishing variety of giraffes, zebras, and their kin that I came to know at Busch Gardens in the 1970s. I also loved the gorillas and polar bears that made an early impression on my career. But, at the end of the day, I'm not sure I have a favorite. It would be like trying to choose a favorite grandchild. I love them all.

I grew up roaming the woods of St. Petersburg, Florida, at a time when the Gulf Coast had wooded areas to roam. My dad worked in construction as a plasterer, so we never had much money. I was the oldest of four boys and served as my dad's chief laborer. I mixed "mud" when he had a side-job plastering someone's walls. I carried a five-gallon bucket and swatted mosquitoes alone in the darkness of some Florida bayou when he was out throwing his cast net on nights when the mullet were running. And I handed him tools when he was under the car repairing the brakes or changing the oil.

I can't think of any defining moments from my childhood that would have predicted the course of my career. We had dogs, and I did love being in the woods—despite the abundance of rattlesnakes. But I was not that child who was always bringing home critters, and we didn't have a zoo in my community. I did, however, study biology at Mercer University in Macon, Georgia. Somehow, that's all it took—that and a chance visit to the zoo in Atlanta in the Spring of 1970.

The trajectory of my career was driven by ambition. I must have had a restless spirit as I moved from job to job, often in spectacular fashion. My first job, for example, came after I gave up the final year of a full-ride college basketball scholarship in Georgia to work as a zookeeper in Tampa. Busch Gardens introduced me to elephants, apes, big cats, and an array of hoofed animals while I pursued my degree in zoology at the University of South Florida.

After two years in Tampa, I landed an exciting position as a senior zookeeper at a new zoo that was being built in Toronto. I arrived in Canada in September 1973—a sunburned Florida cracker ready to face my first Canadian winter without any proper clothing. It was at the Toronto Zoo that I first experienced polar bears and wild-caught baby gorillas. And the Toronto Zoo sent me on the trip of a lifetime to tour the zoos of Europe, followed by a stomach-churning ocean voyage back to Canada.

I was one of a few Americans on a team of zookeepers from Canada, the United Kingdom, Switzerland, Australia, and other parts of the world. I doubt there has ever been a more talented, diverse, and eccentric group of zookeepers assembled anywhere on the planet than those who came together to open the Metro Toronto Zoo. We endured primitive working conditions, low pay, harsh winters, and injuries from wild animals. But the results, at least from my vantage point nearly half a century later, were entirely worth it.

Opening an enormous zoo with thousands of animals was a complex undertaking. With animals arriving daily and their permanent homes still under construction, zoo officials rented holding barns all over the region. Conditions were often alarmingly makeshift. We had a few animal holding spaces on the property, but not nearly enough to accommodate the growing collection. So, on most mornings, zookeepers would strike out in trucks, cars, and even tractors, heading for the temporary holding areas that dotted the countryside—places like the Finch barn, the Johnson barn, the Sedgwick barn, and the old pig farm more than twenty kilometers away in Claremont. We dealt with icy, treacherous winter roads; isolated, lonely locations; and challenging animal medical conditions. We were kicked, bitten, and head-butted, and at the end of the day, we gathered at the Glen Eagles Pub to laugh at our tribulations. We labored long hours at the zoo and spent most evenings at the pub or playing broomball on frozen ponds. I had uprooted my wife and sons, moved them fifteen hundred miles to a foreign country, and proceeded to neglect them as I dove into my new job. It was a great time for my career, but not my finest hour as a father and husband. My marriage began to crumble.

In 1978, I learned that Bob Bean, my old boss from Busch Gardens, was looking for a general curator at his zoo in Louisville, Kentucky. I took the job in hopes that it would advance my career and save my broken marriage. My career flourished. My marriage did not. When my divorce was finalized in 1984, I moved back to Tampa—this time to direct the Lowry Park Zoo and to, once again, help build a new zoo. I also married the love of my life and began a lifelong partnership with Louisville zoo volunteer, Karen Liebert.

The cages I inherited at Lowry Park were mostly chain-link boxes of various sizes that housed lions, tigers, pumas, jaguars, bears, and primates. Two chimpanzees, Herman and Gitta, lived behind iron bars covered with heavy fencing that rendered them almost invisible, while otters and alligators swam in water-filled pits. Shena, the lone elephant, was confined to a small pen with a shelter about the size of a two-car garage.

It was a grim place, but by late 1985, money had been raised and construction began on a new zoo. For nearly three years, workers poured concrete, sculpted artificial rocks, and installed caging until we were finally able to plant grass, test waterfalls, and move animals into their new homes. One of the highlights of my zoo career came in the winter of 1988 when I witnessed Herman and Gitta step out of their new night house and walk on grass for the first time in many years.

Karen and I saw the completion of the Lowry Park Zoo in 1988, then moved to Sioux Falls, South Dakota, where I managed the Great Plains Zoo and Delbridge Museum of Natural History for a couple of years. By that time, we had led two trips to Africa, and she was expecting our first (and my fourth) son. When the Toledo Zoo announced it was looking for a deputy director, we jumped at the chance to move closer to family.

If I had to name a favorite zoo, it would be the Toledo Zoo. When I first visited there in the summer of 1991, it struck me as a unique blend of historic old structures and cutting-edge new animal exhibits. The thirty-acre site was compact and filled with interest. Intense, colorful plantings accentuated the architecture of ornate brick and stone buildings. It billed itself as America's most complete zoo because of its museum, aquarium, and plant conservatory. It had a reputation for developing the latest in immersive zoo exhibits like the African Savanna with its one-of-a-kind Hippoquarium.

From my first project, the three-million-dollar Kingdom of the Apes that opened in 1993, to my final project, the Arctic Encounter that opened in early 2000, Toledo was a whirlwind of animal experiences. I traveled to Africa, South America, and Europe. I encountered Beluga whales and polar bears in the Arctic and stepped over blue-footed boobies in the Galapagos Islands. But after ten years in Toledo, I had the bright idea I wanted to retire from the zoo business and open a home inspection franchise in South Carolina. For some reason, that never took off. Maybe it was a combination of poor business acumen and the fact that the first day of my training took place on 9/11/2001.

The final stop on my zoo odyssey began in June 2004 when I re-entered the zoo world to take over a 700-acre park and zoo in Albany, Georgia, known as Chehaw. We revitalized a small zoo when we brought in black rhinos, flamingos, and cheetahs. I learned the importance of harvesting pine trees sustainably and maintaining the pine savanna woodlands of South Georgia by intentionally setting them on fire. Finally, at the end of 2015, I officially retired and found myself a part-time gig driving a mule wagon at a local quail hunting lodge.

In my career, I have traveled the world working with animals and viewing them in the wild. The number of animals I have encountered is beyond measure. I have watched animals being born and seen them take their last breath. I received animals that were rescued and brought to zoos as orphans from the wild, helped nurse them through sickness, and watched their lives unfold over decades.

I have had an impact on the lives of countless animals at seven different zoos, but they have had an impact on my life, as well. They have quite literally changed my life. So, back to the question, "What is my favorite animal?" I can't name just one, but I can think of ten that are on the short-list.

LESSON 1

Showdown with an Elephant

We faced each other like a couple of gunslingers at high noon. I was armed with a three-foot-long stick called a bull-hook. My opponent had his pair of impressive ivory tusks and six thousand pounds of bulk. Bwana stood about twenty yards away, facing me with his trunk up and his ears fanned out in a threat display. He was a nine-year-old male African elephant who, fortunately for me, was not enraged—at least not yet.

I was a zookeeper at Tampa's Busch Gardens in the early 1970s where the first task on my evening shift as we closed the park, was to help walk five African elephants some two hundred yards from their exhibit in the middle of the African Veldt to their night barn. The elephants were well-trained and the process highly ritualized. We always had at least two handlers, and we began the routine by opening the massive steel gate to their exhibit and calling the five animals by name.

As the elephants ambled through the gate, we told them to "come in line." When we had them lined up in proper order, we commanded, "trunk," then "foot." Once they had each raised their trunk and their right front foot and held their position to our satisfaction—demonstrating that we had control—we could begin our walk to the barn with the commands, "all right" followed by "go on away."

It was an ordered march by silent beasts and mostly silent men ambling like ghosts through the humid evening air. I scarcely noticed as zebras raised their heads and giraffes stopped to watch us pass. I was a young man barely out of my teens, but after just a few months, I had grown accustomed to having these massive, dangerous beasts obey my commands. Perhaps it was some natural, in-born pride, but I liked the feeling of power and gave little thought to how I had come to be there.

A few years before my encounter with Bwana, I was completing my junior year at Mercer University in Macon, Georgia, on a basketball scholarship. Though I was studying biology, I had no idea what I wanted to pursue upon graduation.

Lessons from the Zoo

Every spring, a few of my teammates and I made the two-hour drive north to Fulton County Stadium for an Atlanta Braves baseball game. Those trips came with some time to fill, so we often found ourselves exploring a unique shopping and entertainment district in downtown Atlanta. The area dated from the late nineteenth and early twentieth centuries, when a series of viaducts were built in the city-center to bridge the railroad tracks and relieve congestion. Atlanta continued to grow above these viaducts—and above the original street level—until the ground floors of these buildings were essentially sealed off and forgotten. In the 1960s, they were rediscovered and developed as Underground Atlanta.

I don't recall why we changed our routine, but on one of our baseball trips, we decided to do something different. Someone suggested a side-trip that was much closer to the stadium—the Atlanta Zoo. This was a life-changing experience for me. I had never been to a zoo, and I was well and truly hooked by the experience. I marveled at the elephants, big cats, and Atlanta's famous gorilla, Willie B. I was amazed at the variety of creatures in the zoo's state-of-the-art World of Reptiles, a facility that would stand until it was replaced forty-four years later. The Atlanta Zoo was not one of the world's great zoos, but it was good enough to lure me into a career caring for animals.

When I returned to school, I couldn't get the zoo and its animals out of my mind. Though I was tall at six feet, eight inches, my athletic ability was limited. I was never going to be a professional basketball player. That summer, I gave up the final year of my basketball scholarship, transferred to the University of South Florida in Tampa to study zoology, and found a job at Busch Gardens.

Busch Gardens opened in the late 1950s as a beer-tasting area adjacent to Tampa's Anheuser-Busch Brewery. Guests were lured to a brewery tour with the promise of a free glass of beer and a visit to one of the most beautiful and unique botanical gardens in America. Visitors could meander through acres of lush plantings and view hundreds of colorful, raucous tropical birds.

In the mid-1960s, Busch Gardens expanded its attraction to include a monorail ride through a large expanse of sandy, open land that resembled the Serengeti Plains of Africa. It was, as I recall, a hundred or so acres of hoofed animal pastures divided by long, meandering waterways. The larger, dangerous animals were contained behind deep, hidden dry moats. I did not realize it at the time but, while every other zoo in America held its animals in small cages, wire pens, and brick buildings, Busch Gardens had opened one of the best zoos in the world. I was fortunate to receive my early training at a zoo that was far ahead of its time.

Lessons from the Zoo

My first job at Busch Gardens was hosing debris and duck poop from what seemed like miles of sidewalks that wound through the gardens. This was followed by a stint as a monorail driver before I landed that coveted position in the zoo department in the fall of 1971.

Shortly after I began working as a zookeeper at Busch Gardens, I was interviewed for an article in the *St. Petersburg Times* Sunday magazine, *The Floridian*. The article, entitled "New Zoos for Everyone, Bar None," explored the place of zoos in the 1970s and suggested that the very essence of our fascination with animals begins when we are children.

Children, the reporter noted, adore zoos in ways that adults can't because children don't know that the animals are in cages. Once we begin to recognize the barriers, we develop an uneasiness in our attitude toward zoos. Then, we begin to debate whether they are educational and useful, or they are cruel and inhumane. The article also recognized a new purpose for zoos—public education, scientific study, and the preservation of endangered species.

I suppose the reporter chose to interview me because I was an idealistic, twenty-two-year-old zoology student who was preparing for a career in zoo management. The article described me as a sensitive young man, suggesting that my life revolved around a love of animals and a belief that zoos should transform themselves from menageries into relevant institutions in American society. The reporter seemed to recognize that my job elicited passion and compassion, but also a good measure of excitement and danger.

Here is how I described my job in a March 1973 letter of application for a position at another zoo:

> *For the last 16 months I have worked the 4:00–midnight shift in order that I might pursue my studies in the daytime. The first part of my night is involved in feeding and returning all display animals to their nighttime quarters. My partner and I are responsible for lions, leopards, cheetahs, river and pigmy hippos, black and white rhinos, Cape buffaloes, baboons, gorillas, chimpanzees, gibbons, and okapi. Myself and two other men are responsible for walking the large male and four female African elephants to their nighttime quarters. The remainder of my evening is spent alone, patrolling pastures and inspecting herds of giraffe, zebra, antelope, and gazelles. Often my responsibilities include assisting in difficult births, bottle-feeding babies who can't nurse, assisting the zoo veterinarian, and effecting emergency repairs on equipment whenever necessary.*

The zoo business was about to undergo a remarkable renaissance in the 1970s and, as my luck would have it, that is when I arrived on the scene. As I began my zoo career, cities all over North America were transforming their zoos. In San Diego, California, for example, a wild animal park opened in 1972 on nearly 2,000 acres of property. It was the result of a decade of planning by zoo officials who wanted to see their animals exhibited in natural environments instead of cages.

Also, in 1972, the city of Miami had plans for a new zoo. They were prompted by a hurricane that devastated the old Crandon Park Zoo in 1965. Construction of a new, 600-acre zoo on the site of an abandoned naval air station began in 1975. At the same time, folks in Minneapolis were looking at a 500-acre site for a new zoo in the suburb of Apple Valley. Their goal was to replace traditional steel bars with cutting-edge designs—open exhibits, naturalistic settings, and glass barriers.

In Canada, the City of Toronto was closing its outdated zoo in Riverdale Park and building a new $28 million zoo on an impressive site thirty miles outside of town. The property consisted of 310 acres of tableland and 400 acres of forest in the Rouge River Valley. The new Metro Toronto Zoo would be the next stop on my zoo journey. I could not know it at the time, but I was in for a remarkable ride.

The oldest American zoos were celebrating their centennial anniversaries and, after a hundred years of operation, they had changed hardly at all. In the next few decades, I would witness zoos discontinue the centuries-old practice of man-handling elephants like Bwana in favor of a safer, more humane practice called protected contact. I would oversee the training of apes to submit to routine medical screenings. I would see zoos begin to spend more on one exhibit than the City of Toronto spent on its entire 710-acre zoo. And, most remarkably, I would witness zoo professionals begin to unravel the mysteries of animal communication.

As zoos in the 1970s found themselves having to answer for the conditions in which they kept their animals, my experience as a new zookeeper was limited. At that time, I had a vision of what zoos should be, but I also knew of the controversial study of more than seventy public and private zoos made the previous year by the Humane Society of the United States (HSUS). Syndicated columnist Jack Anderson had given the report wide publicity. The investigator for the HSUS, Sue Pressman, found inhumane conditions in almost a quarter of the facilities she inspected.

Animal welfare issues were also being recognized by federal regulators. In December 1970, legislation was passed under the Animal Welfare Act to include all warm-blooded animals determined by the Secretary of Agriculture as being used or intended for use in experimentation or exhibition. Exhibitors (including zoos) were incorporated into the act, research facilities were defined, and regular inspections were proposed. The laws would be enforced by the USDA and its Secretary was directed to develop regulations regarding record keeping and the humane care and treatment of animals in or during commerce, exhibition, experimentation, and transport.

These were the practical aspects of improving the conditions for animals in zoos. But there was another dimension, a non-practical, even spiritual dimension which those of us who had daily contact with zoo animals recognized. It was evident from my interview that I felt it, but I scarcely recognized it myself. I was, according to the interview, maintaining contact with my biological heritage, experiencing the power of wildness in an almost mystical way. And it complicated the debate over the continued existence of zoos. I loved my job and wanted—or needed—to be around the animals. I was, apparently, unwilling or unable to admit that the reasons I gave in defense of zoos were less a description of reality than a vision of what I thought zoos could and should become.

The change in zoos during the next two decades would surpass all advances in zoos for the previous two centuries. But in order to appreciate how great the transition was, we need to go back to the beginning when zoos were menageries that traveled with the circus and its most iconic of circus animals—the elephant.

Sometime in 1861, at the beginning of the American Civil War, a baby African elephant was captured not long after his birth. He was sold to an animal dealer, transported across the Mediterranean, and ended up at the *Jardin des Plantes* in Paris. The French agreed to exchange the unremarkable elephant, and in 1865, he was shipped to England. The little elephant was in poor physical condition but his trainer, Matthew Scott, nursed him back to health and named him Jumbo. He eventually reached a height of about twelve feet at the shoulder and a weight of about seven tons. Jumbo became a popular fixture at the London Zoo.

In 1881, Jumbo came to the attention of circus magnate P. T. Barnum. Jumbo's size had become legendary, and Barnum wanted to acquire the biggest elephant in the world. He offered to purchase Jumbo from the zoo for ten thousand dollars. The zoo agreed, but under pressure from the public, tried to revoke the sale. Barnum refused.

In March 1882, after considerable difficulty, Jumbo was packed into an enormous crate and left England for America. He arrived in New York on April 9 with much fanfare, and the next day, he was displayed at Madison Square Garden. Jumbo spent the next three years crisscrossing the continent, transported in his own train car. He drew huge crowds for Barnum, even though he performed no tricks like the other elephants. His mere presence was enough.

Jumbo's story came to a tragic end at 9:30 p.m. on September 15, 1885, when Jumbo and another smaller elephant named Tom Thumb were being moved from the circus grounds in St. Thomas, Ontario, Canada to their train. At the same time, Special Freight train #151 was barreling down a parallel track out of sight of the elephants and their handlers. As the elephants crossed the track, the engineer, William Burnip, saw the elephants, sounded the warning horn, and put the train into reverse. It screeched to a halt—but it was too late. The train hit Tom Thumb first and tossed him into a nearby ravine. Jumbo was struck on his hind end, causing the train to derail. His injuries were fatal.

Five years after Jumbo's tragic death, the city that had lured me into the zoo business began its search for an elephant to add to its recently opened zoo. In early 1890, the Atlanta newspaper established an Elephant Fund to encourage donations, a New York broker was hired, and several elephants were discussed. A twelve-year-old female Asian elephant was finally located in Germany and was purchased in July by the *Atlanta Constitution* newspaper.

After her purchase, she was loaded onto a ship and delivered to the port of Philadelphia on July 31, 1890. Five days later, a train pulled into Atlanta's Piedmont Park and the elephant made a short walk to her temporary enclosure, where she enjoyed a week's rest after her long journey. According to reports, she was a fine, well-trained animal that could also carry a howdah for riding children. The elaborate transfer to her permanent home from Piedmont Park to Grant Park was planned for Thursday, August 14, with a parade. After walking through downtown Atlanta, the elephant turned left on Mitchell Street and marched past Georgia's new state capitol building before turning down Hill Street and Milledge Avenue.

Zoo Atlanta's first elephant walked into Grant Park by way of Milledge Avenue on an August afternoon in 1890. According to the *Atlanta Constitution*, she was very tired after the long march through the "dust and dearth" of the six-mile route. At the zoo, a space had been prepared in the new zoo building near the main entrance. It was said to have been neatly floored with stout planks and had windows on either side to admit light and air. Instead of a fence, a huge post had been driven into the ground, to which she would be fastened.

Unlike most of the large, dangerous animals in these early zoos and circuses, elephants engendered an amazing amount of trust. Elephants walked untethered down crowd-lined streets. They carried children on their backs. They were even put to work as unpaid laborers, erecting tents and carrying heavy loads. I witnessed this mutual trust firsthand when I worked with Bwana, Elke, and the other elephants at Tampa's Busch Gardens. And I witnessed trust a dozen years later when I assumed responsibility for another elephant across town at an aging zoo in Tampa's Lowry Park.

Lessons from the Zoo

A few days after Christmas 1960, Sumter Lowry Jr. presented a special Christmas gift to the city of Tampa. Lowry had purchased a baby elephant from Thailand. Her arrival was front-page news. In February 1961, she was given the name Shena, compliments of a public naming contest. She was just eighteen months old when she arrived at Tampa's Lowry Park Zoo.

In the years that followed, a modest building was constructed to serve as a shelter. Her small yard was surrounded by railroad rails that were welded to concrete pillars. There she would live for the next two decades until I arrived in 1984 and helped develop a new master plan that called for the demolition of her exhibit and the construction of a new, larger space in the same location. In order to build her new facilities, she would need to be moved to another zoo for a few years.

After searching far and wide, we found a good facility at African Lion Safari near Toronto, Canada, that would take her. They had proper facilities, other elephants, and a highly competent staff. A deal was struck that would send her to Canada and bring her back when her new home was completed. All we had to do was figure out how to get her there. I described the process in my article for the zoo's newsletter in the fall of 1985:

Though highly trained, Shena had not been handled in over ten years. She had become quite unmanage-

able and even dangerous to those who worked around her. But after a few days with [an] experienced elephant handler, she was performing all of her old tricks and even seemed to enjoy the change in routine and the companionship of her handler. The next problem was how to get her out of the enclosure. So complete was Shena's incarceration, that there was not even a gate into her enclosure. Our friendly workmen moved in with their cutting torches and bulldozers, and after nearly an hour of cutting the heavy iron rails, an opening was made in the pen.

The next problem we faced was the uncertainty of Shena's reactions to her newfound freedom. Would she respond to her handler's commands, or would she run away at the first opportunity? The moment of truth arrived. As Shena walked out of her pen for the first time in nearly 15 years, it became obvious that she was happy to be outside and yet very responsive to her handler. She quickly gained his confidence and was soon allowed to wander happily around and explore the zoo she had lived in for most of her life. The rest of her loading and transporting was so uneventful as to appear routine. But that was not the end of the story.

In order to make transportation less traumatic, another elephant was brought from Canada to keep her company. A large male Asian elephant named

Lessons from the Zoo

"Buke" became the first elephant ever to share Shena's enclosure. Though she was coy to his advances at first and turned her back whenever he came close, she soon warmed up and remained close by his side as they explored the zoo grounds.

At the time of Shena's transfer, the zoo had been cleared for construction and most of the cages and sidewalks were gone. We trusted the elephants enough to allow them some freedom. They had space to wander, plenty of sand to throw on themselves, and few opportunities to get into trouble. Buke was an impressive beast with massive tusks. He seemed calm enough, responding to his handlers like an anxious child as the two elephants wandered the property untethered. He was so gentle that I took a photo of my twelve-year-old son, Jason, riding on his back.

The next time I saw Buke was at his home in Canada later that summer. He was in musth (a period when bull elephants are sexually active and extremely aggressive) and chained to a tree—ready to kill anyone who came too near.

Shena did well in Canada, and we were pleased later that summer when we learned that breeding was taking place. Our hopes were dashed, however, when we received word that she had died of heart failure on January 17, 1986. We should not have been surprised.

Elephants in the wild walk for miles every day. They thrive on exercise. Shena's exercise for the past few decades in Tampa had been limited to the small enclosure she inhabited. Though it had been gratifying to see her roam the zoo site with Buke and travel to Canada where she could spend her days with other elephants, I suspect the sudden burst of activity and interaction with other elephants that resulted from her move to Canada was probably more than her debilitated heart could handle. The only consolation was that the last few months of her life were probably some of her happiest.

When I arrived at my first zoo job and began to work with the elephants at Busch Gardens, they were already trained. It wasn't until many years later, when I met an elephant named Jana at the Louisville Zoo, that I learned how elephants were trained in those days. Jana was about two years old—the by-product of extensive culling operations in southern Africa. She came to us from a holding compound in Ohio where she had been living with twenty or so other babies and she needed to be trained for a life in captivity.

To be trained in those days, meant "broken," or tamed for human contact. She would be taught various commands, not unlike housebreaking a dog to live indoors. She would learn to trust her human handlers, and they would learn to trust her in return.

Lessons from the Zoo

To accomplish this training, the zoo hired legendary circus man and elephant trainer Robert "Smokey" Jones. At the time, Smokey was in his mid-fifties—a gruff, no-nonsense bear of a man who lived in a camper near the hay barn. His methods of training were rough, but he did get results, and at the time, we wouldn't have known of any other way to do it. Jana was completely wild.

I wasn't there for most of the actual training, but I do know he was successful because she eventually learned to follow our directions and worked her way into our system. I am guessing that the elephants I worked with at Busch Gardens would have been trained in that manner.

The Busch Gardens elephants walked in single file every evening after we brought them out of their enclosure. Their trunks held the tails of the individual in front as they were led by a dependable old female named Elke. Evening after evening, we ambled through a pasture occupied by zebra, giraffe, and other hoofed stock without incident—except on those occasions when Bwana decided to break out of line. His usual tactic was to run a few yards away, wheel around to face his handlers, and fan out his ears in a threat display. He dared us to approach him. On those evenings when I was the lead handler, it was my job to walk slowly toward him, calming him with the command, "Bwana, steady," grab the massive animal by the tusk, and tell him to "move up" and "come in line."

At roughly the same time I was facing off with Bwana, on a Saturday afternoon in June 1972, a similar face-off was occurring in the small town of Issoire, in south-central France. No one knows what touched off the incident, but Chiquita, an adult Asian elephant, attacked her trainer and began charging at everything in sight. People ran for their lives as the animal smashed tents, overturned wagons, and trumpeted her outrage.

The Rancy Circus was no small-time mom-and-pop affair. An elaborate, colorful poster (ca. 1972) advertised a "Zoo" with one-hundred-sixty animals. When circus owner, forty-three-year-old Dany Renz-Chanon, tried to calm the elephant, she attacked him, too. According to reports from the chaotic scene, when Renz-Chanon hid under a wagon, the elephant overturned the caravan and trampled the man, killing him on the spot. Although news reports claimed that other circus hands managed to get the elephant under control, a circus history website says Chiquita was euthanized later that day.

As Bwana warily watched me approach, he was probably looking for subtle threats—a faltering voice, a sudden move, a raised stick. He was deciding whether to trust me. I was taught to show no fear and to be firm and commanding, but my heart thumped as I considered what I would do if he refused my orders. He never did. It was only later in my career, after numerous reports of elephants like

Chiquita killing their handlers, that I came to appreciate what a dangerous profession I had chosen.

Sadly, Bwana would only live another two years before he died of a viral infection. As far as I know, he never hurt anybody. He taught me that when we are dealing with animals, we are judged by our actions. They don't care about our polished appearance or our smooth-talking. I believe that the most precious thing in this world is trust. It can take years to earn, only a matter of seconds to lose, and once lost impossible to regain. It calls to mind a powerful quote I once heard. *I'm not upset that you lied to me, I'm upset that from now on I can't believe you.*

I trusted Bwana and I believe he trusted me. Working with massive animals like elephants taught me how important lesson number one—trust—can be. But it also filled me with hubris at having these powerful animals obey my commands. It would take an encounter with a lion to bring that hubris back into balance and teach me lesson number two.

LESSON 2

Close Call with a Big Cat

It was a common mistake for a new zookeeper, but it was nearly a fatal one. I had opened the door to the lion's cage and stepped inside to place a bowl of meat for his evening feed. As I put down the bowl, I glanced at the shift door to the adjacent cage where the lion awaited his meal. The door was open, and I could see him lying in the next cage. My heart raced as I moved quickly to get out and slam the gate. The fear and shame at how careless I had been made me slightly nauseous, but I quietly set the lock and glanced down the hall toward Thornell Floyd. He was the experienced keeper who was responsible for my training. He did not see what I had just done, and

I never told him. I didn't want my career to be over before it had begun.

The big cat ambled into the cage I had just vacated and began his evening meal, unaware of the valuable lesson I had just learned and the powerful impact he would have on my career. For the next forty years, I would check and double-check locks and follow other safety measures to ensure that no harm came to me or my animals.

The lions at Busch Gardens in the 1970s lived in a remote section of the park. Visitors observed them from the safety of an electric monorail ride as it glided through the veldt a few times every hour. The prey animals (zebras, giraffes, and antelope) were separated from the family of lions that inhabited their small, rocky outcrop by a deep concrete pit encircling their area. It was in fact an island.

My job as the night keeper was to begin my shift by teaming with someone at the end of his day shift to bring animals into shelters for the night. The lions presented a unique challenge because the access for keepers was down a small elevator to a cramped tunnel that took us under the bottom of the dry moat, some twenty feet underground, and back up another elevator into the lions' night house.

The holding area we entered was a dimly lit hallway about thirty feet long with cages along both sides. When we came up the elevator into the holding area, we were contained inside a steel cage that afforded us a view of the hallway. We could see that all the cage doors were closed, and the locks secured.

The cages had been cleaned during the day and were ready to receive the lions. All we had to do was open a sliding door to allow the animals to enter an empty cage, place meat into an adjacent cage, and shift the lions into the cage that contained their food. That is when I messed up.

Thornell Floyd (or Floyd, as he preferred to be called) was a stickler for safety, which made my blunder all the more egregious. After we were finished feeding the animals every evening and all the cages were securely locked, he insisted that we both pull on every padlock in the building. He went down the line pulling locks, and I went right behind him. It seemed silly at the time but when we left that building, we both knew it was secure. It was a valuable lesson in how important it was to be slow and deliberate when dealing with dangerous animals.

As my career advanced, I discovered that having a partner to back me up was not a common occurrence. At other zoos, I often worked alone. I frequently did not have the luxury of having a team member to check my locks, and I recall countless evenings at home trying to remember if I did lock a lock. I also read many accounts of zookeepers and volunteers being injured and killed by big cats.

After Floyd and I completed our rounds, I worked alone to feed and secure the rest of the animals. These were animals that were either nonthreatening or animals I did not enter cages to feed. One such animal was the quiet female African leopard, who would remain timidly snarling at the back of her night quarters every evening when I shoved her meat under the bars of her cage. One evening, the empty meat bag slipped out of my hand and landed in the gutter that ran along the front of her cage. When I casually reached down to retrieve it, she bolted from the back of the cage in the blink of an eye and grabbed my hand with her claws. Fortunately for me, she only got me with one claw, which dug into the fleshy part of my left hand, leaving a scar that reminds me of that close call to this day.

Another close encounter with a big cat occurred later in my career when I was General Curator of the Louisville Zoo. We were preparing to open a new exhibit for Siberian tigers and had three animals to transfer from a temporary holding area to their new exhibit. On May 29, 1979, we attempted the transfer but were only able to coax a female named Morgana to walk into the crate for transfer. According to my notes, the other female, Tanya, fought tooth and nail, and the male, Sergei, simply refused to move. The next day, we brought in a veterinary team with tranquilizer darts, and Tanya went down in seven minutes and was transferred without incident. Sergei was another story.

He was darted but only became drowsy. He refused to go down. The vet gave him more drugs, first through the bars with a pole syringe, then through a carefully opened door by hand injection. I have participated in hundreds of these procedures we called "knock-downs" in my career. They were often tedious affairs punctuated by long minutes of watching animals become drowsy in some dim, concrete holding area. We passed the time by telling stories and talking about current events.

When we thought Sergei was asleep, I entered the cage with two other keepers, Dave Marshall and Ray Doyle. But when we began to tie his feet together in anticipation of dragging him into a crate, he woke up and chased the three of us out of the cage with a throaty growl. We had to wait an additional twenty-minutes for him to relaxed enough for us to complete the transfer. We were also able to get an accurate weight on Sergei. He weighed in at an intimidating four-hundred pounds. An operation that should have taken a few minutes took two hours and included one awfully close call.

I have never been much of a cat person. I was raised with dogs and was never around cats until I came to work with them in zoos. The only cats I knew were either threatening my life or outright attacking me. Then one day a few years ago, a skinny black cat wandered into our garage. My wife and I warned our son not to feed the cat, but he felt sorry for her. We named her Binney (after the city in which we lived—Albany or Al-Binney) after she insinuated herself into our lives. Even the dogs came to tolerate her presence in our house. Bexley mostly ignored the cat, but Chelsea and Binney sparred playfully. Chelsea would stick her nose to Binney's face and Binney swatted Chelsea with her clawless pads.

Binney exhibited none of those characteristics that cats are known for. She was not aloof or disdainful of our presence. She was friendly. She liked to be stroked. She was good with the dogs, and she enriched our lives as part of the family. She helped me see what cat-people see in cats and why some cats—especially lions—are so popular. Lions star in films like *Clarence the Cross-eyed Lion* (1965), *Born Free* (1966), *The Lion King* (1994), and *The Ghost and the Darkness* (1996). They are also common in literature, for example, *The Lion, the Witch, and the Wardrobe* by C. S. Lewis, *Cry of the Kalahari*, by Mark Owens, and *The Man-eaters of Tsavo*, a true story published in 1907 by John Henry Patterson.

For nine months in 1898, according to Patterson's book, workers on the British Kenya-Uganda Railway were terrorized, attacked, and eaten by two enormous lions. At least thirty-five people, and possibly as many as one-hundred thirty-five (depending on the source), were killed by the stealthy lions the natives named "Ghost" and "Darkness."

The railway project was intended to link Mombasa, Kenya to Lake Victoria in Uganda in order to create a trade route for raw materials and British goods into Uganda. The project relied on the skills of thousands of imported Sikh laborers from British India along with local laborers, but the project came to a halt from March to December after the two lions began picking off workers. Efforts to barricade work camps failed, and the work crew became increasingly terrified.

Tsavo lions are different from savanna lions. They are exceptionally large, and the males are often maneless. Their behavior in the wild is also different, and, in those days, they may have become accustomed to seeing humans as easy prey following years of having slave trains pass through their territory and feasting on the bodies of the dead that were tossed off the trains.

It fell to railway engineer J. H. Patterson to stalk and kill the man-eaters. Patterson was a skilled hunter, but not a professional marksman. He finally tracked and killed the lions in December 1898 and reportedly sold their bodies for $5,000 to the Field Museum in Chicago.

It was in Kenya's Tsavo National Park, not far from where Patterson had killed the man-eaters, that I first saw lions in the wild in March 1986. My wife and I were enjoying our first night sleeping in the African bush when we heard a commotion outside our room. Sometime after midnight, a massive herd of Cape buffalo moved into the dimly lit waterhole about one-hundred feet from our porch. We could hear them bellow and splash about, but we were content to try to sleep. At about 4 a.m., however, we both sprang from bed at the same time. We had heard a roar. We fumbled for our binoculars and crept out to the porch. We heard the roar again and spotted four female lions. Two were stalking a young buffalo and two lions were further back. The herd bull charged the two stalkers, and the lions backed off. This went on for about twenty minutes before the buffalo herd moved off into the night. They didn't flee in a blind panic, but they weren't ambling as easily as when they had arrived. It was more like they had suddenly remembered someplace they had to be. As the last of the herd disappeared down the path into the darkness, the lions followed, and the drama was over—at least for us.

After things quieted down, Karen went back to bed and I sat alone on the porch for a while. Hundreds of bats fluttered about, catching bugs that were attracted to the lights that illuminated the waterhole. About five minutes after the buffalo left, the frogs in the waterhole began calling. My hearing had grown acute as I sat in the darkness. I heard a sound off to my left that sounded like a distant roar. I wondered if the lions had caught up to the buffalo. I heard the roar again, this time more clearly. It was the man in the next cabin, snoring. Time for me to go back to bed.

A few days later, in Amboseli National Park, we happened upon another pride of lions. They were not on the prowl. They were asleep in the shade of an Acacia tree draped over an old termite mound. We snapped a few photos and prepared to move on but were halted by a small drama that developed. Across from us on the other side of the termite mound was another safari vehicle. Its occupants had been sitting on the roof of the vehicle on some cushions, but when they slipped back down the hatch into their vehicle, one of the cushions blew off and landed a few feet from the lions. The lions took no notice, but we sensed something might be about to unfold. It appeared that the occupants of the vehicle wanted to retrieve their cushion.

We watched as the vehicle moved into position and the lions continued to doze. We could see a stick being waved around inside the vehicle. Would the driver be foolish enough to get out and attempt to retrieve the cushion? The vehicle stopped, the driver held up his stick and clicked the door open. That was all it took. The sound of the door brought all the lions to full alert. After a few moments of indecision, the vehicle drove off, leaving the cushion behind.

The most dramatic indication of how lions in the wild operate came during our second visit to Africa in March 1989. We were in Kenya's Aberdare National Park, staying at an iconic lodge called the Ark. It is modeled in appearance after Noah's Ark, and it overlooks a floodlit waterhole and salt lick. It has multiple viewing decks and attracts a host of awesome wildlife. We had spent the night watching herds of elephants, warthogs, and hoofed stock come and go, but the excitement really began after breakfast as we were preparing to depart. Someone spotted two female lions lurking at the edge of the woods surrounding the waterhole. Everyone at the lodge gathered at the overlook in anticipation of what might happen. We were not to be disappointed.

When a young bushbuck antelope appeared from the forest that surrounded the waterhole and cautiously moved into the open, people scrambled for their cameras. When they saw the bushbuck, one of the lions separated and circled closer to the lodge. The bushbuck was cautious, moving and stopping to peer at his surroundings and moving again. The lion continued to circle, pausing when the bushbuck paused. The lion was in position when the bushbuck arrived at the waterhole. We held our breath when it became obvious what was about to happen.

As the bushbuck lowered his head to drink, the lion lunged and sent it running back toward the forest—right into the waiting jaws of her partner, who had remained concealed until the last moment. The lion grabbed the bushbuck by the throat as it passed her and gave it a mighty shake. She then dragged the limp prey back into the bush where the two lions would feast, as we left for the next stop on our tour. It was an extraordinary display of instinctive teamwork and patience, and a powerful illustration of how the natural world operates.

Old-school zoo men who operated in the early years of the twentieth century were not at all averse to the thrill and danger of entering cages with bears, hyenas, or lions. The director of Chicago's Lincoln Park Zoo around the turn of the twentieth century, Cyrus DeVry, for example, seemed to relish entering pens with dangerous animals. He was known to enter cages and break up fights or move dangerous animals with nothing more than a club.

When I began working at the Toledo Zoo in the 1990s, I had a glimpse of how these old-school zoo men must have kept and handled their lions and other big cats. One of the first buildings that caught my eye had the word *CARNIVORA* etched in the stone lintel above the door. Its stucco walls and red clay-tiled roof were in the Spanish colonial style. The building was more like a cathedral than an animal house with its soaring facade, arched glass windows, and ornate stone carvings. Officials broke ground on the building known as the Lion House in 1924, with Theodore Roosevelt's son Kermit turning the first shovel of dirt, and it opened to the public on Christmas Day, 1927. Similar buildings were in fashion at zoos all around the country. The Toledo Zoo's original lion house opened in 1907 but was demolished when the newer one was built. The Lincoln Park Zoo in Chicago opened its Lion House in 1912. It featured an impressive great hall with a vaulted ceiling and clerestory windows. It was said to be a much larger version of the lion house at the London Zoo.

These historic lion houses were lined with stark, iron-barred cages that were not particularly conducive to the health and well-being of the animals but allowed the visitors a good view of the inhabitants. The purpose of their cages was to offer the best view of the animals. By the time I began my zoo career, zoos were phasing out these old buildings.

Most modern zoos, especially the accredited ones, are also removing the keepers from direct contact with dangerous animals. But accidents are still going to happen. A door will be left unlocked, a hand will get too close to a cage, or an animal will make an unprecedented leap.

I am reminded of my close calls every time I learn of the death of another animal handler, like my friend Dave Marshall. Dave was killed in June 1994 by a three-hundred fifty-pound Bengal tiger named Lucknow while working as a senior zookeeper at the Metrozoo in Miami, Florida. Dave was a friend and a fellow zookeeper who had helped me wrestle a groggy, male Siberian tiger fifteen years earlier at the Louisville Zoo. He was apparently working alone and made a fatal mistake—not unlike the mistake I had made two decades earlier.

Those of us in the profession know how dangerous our dream job can be. We are in daily contact with animals that can kill us—big cats, bears, elephants, killer whales, venomous snakes—and we wouldn't have it any other way. It is what we do. These animals depend on us for their survival, and we accept the inherent risk that goes with daily contact. But it is risk, I have come to learn, that is tempered with caution.

Lesson number two is stated in many ways. In the fable about the tortoise and the hare, it is slow and steady wins the race. The old carpenter's maxim is measure twice and cut once. Many of the animals I worked with during my career were dangerous and even deadly, but an encounter with a lion during my first few weeks as a zookeeper taught me a valuable lesson in how important it was to be slow and deliberate when dealing with dangerous animals.

Fortunately, though, my job was not all risk and danger. I spent some of my most enjoyable hours with animals that were not trying to harm me—animals like a couple of opinionated mules named Thelma and Louise.

LESSON 3

A Trailblazing Mule

I began my career at Busch Gardens in 1971 surrounded by hoofed animals in the African Veldt—giraffes, zebras, and more species of antelope and gazelle than I can remember. So, it was fitting that in my retirement more than four decades later, I once again found myself working with hoofed animals as a part-time mule wagon driver at a local quail hunting lodge.

In their heyday, mules were as common as trucks are today. As a young boy, my dad plowed his family farm behind a mule. Twenty-mule teams hauled tons of borax out of Death Valley, California. Mules dragged cannons across the Western Front in World War I and served as pack animals in the Burma

Campaign of World War II. On the home front, mules were used to pull wagons and farm implements until the 1930s, when they were replaced by motorized tractors and trucks.

Today, mules are more of a novelty. Everyone has heard the expression "stubborn as a mule," but few people have spent time with mules. In my time driving the mule wagon, I have come to appreciate the mules for their strength, their patience, and their intelligence. As to their stubbornness, perhaps there is another way to view that trait.

When I was grooming the mules in the morning and one of the eight or ten horses at the hitching post wandered too near, I could easily push the horse out of my way. If my mules, on the other hand, were out of position and I wanted to move them, I not only could not push them, they pushed back. I got the impression they were not so much stubborn as they were opinionated. They just did not like being told what to do.

As a wagon driver, my workday began before sunrise after the horses and mules had been brought into the barn from the pasture. My first order of business was to grab the bridles from the tack room and see which stall my mules had wandered into—usually the last stall on the right (mules must be creatures of habit, too).

Because entering the fifteen-foot by fifteen-foot stall with a couple of animals that weigh nearly a thousand pounds could be challenging in the dim light of a predawn morning, I carried a few mule treats in my pocket. That would usually lure them to the front of the stall where I could slip the bit into their mouths and tug their considerable ears through the headpieces. Once I buckled their chin straps and grabbed their leads, they followed me out to the hitching post like a couple of dogs on their morning walk.

The amount of time spent brushing and grooming depended on which mules I was driving. Thelma and Louise had longer coats and required more effort to brush the dried mud, small twigs, and oak leaves out of their fur. Bert and Ernie, on the other hand, were a couple of short-haired grays and nothing seemed to stick to them.

The harness for the mules came in two parts. First, I fastened the padded leather collar around their necks. Then I tossed the rest of the apparatus—fifty pounds of leather straps, metal buckles, and chains—over their backs. It took a good ten minutes to stretch out the harness on the mule's back; sort out the chains and straps; and get it buckled, strapped, and hooked into place. When hitched to the wagon, the mules pulled from a hook under their collar fastened to the front tongue of the wagon and two chain traces running down each of their sides and fastened to the wagon at their rears.

My grandparents must have gone through a similar process every time they wanted to go somewhere. As for me, I've grown so lazy and accustomed to my car's keyless ignition that I get annoyed when I need to dig a key out of my pocket to drive a car. Patience, it seems, is something of a lost art.

When they were in-harness and ready to pull, and I gave the command to "giddy-up," Louise (the right-side mule) jerked forward to get the wagon started. That was about the only work she did all day. The rest of the time, it was Thelma's harness that was taut from pulling and it was Thelma that arrived back at the barn at the end of the day covered in sweat. Louise was as fresh as a vine-ripened tomato—no sweat, no heavy breathing, and eager to get out to the pasture for her evening graze.

Thelma and Louise were about seventeen years old, which put them in their prime in mule years. The mules on the other wagon were each twenty-seven and, with a life expectancy of around thirty years, were nearing the end of their wagon-pulling days. That is why we needed to break-in some new mules—a couple of light-gray, short-haired, seven-year-old males I called Bert and Ernie.

Bert worked on my left and was the steady one—much like Thelma. Ernie, on the other hand, was skittish. When I first attempted to drive through the open wagon shed so I could park the wagon at the end of the day, he suspiciously eyed the coiled hose, the garbage can, and the pallet of supplies on our right side and eased to his left, pushing Bert out of line. I had to stop the wagon and have someone pull the mules forward and into position. One evening, as we were driving in at the end of the day, we encountered a basketball-sized pile of Spanish moss lying in the middle of the road. The horses stepped over it without hesitation, but Ernie saw it before I did and cocked his head, looking at it nervously. The nearer we got, the higher he raised his head until he began to push Bert to the left into the tall grass at the edge of the road. No amount of tugging on the reins could pull them back in line. Thankfully, there were no trees or ditches in our new path, and I was able to wrangle them back into the road when the "danger" was safely passed.

Bert and Ernie came in at different times, so they were not a true pair of pulling mules that could work together. This was most evident when I asked them to "giddy-up," and they pulled sideways in different directions. If I was not careful, they would even begin to back up. Eventually, after a lot of persuasion on my part, one of them would jerk forward and another uncertain journey began.

There are times when I wonder if Oliver Wendell Holmes Jr. had me in mind when he quipped, "You will never appreciate the potentialities of the English language until you have heard a southern mule driver search the soul of a mule."

When I worked there, Busch Gardens was noted for its impressive and diverse collection of hoofed animals. As a night keeper, much of my time was spent patrolling the pastures, counting heads, and simply observing them. I learned to distinguish between Grant's gazelles, Thompson's gazelles, and springbok. I could correctly identify two types of zebra, three types of giraffe, and more than a dozen types of antelope and gazelle. I marveled at how they stayed together in herds of their own species. How, when fierce summer rainstorms came up, they all stood facing away from the storm with their butts to the wind. But when they were resting during the night, no two animals faced in the same direction. Collectively, they could see danger approaching from all directions. I saw female giraffes give birth standing up, allowing the newborn to plop to the ground from several feet in the air. I learned that baby wildebeest would run with the herd just minutes after birth, but baby Thompson's gazelles could not. The strategy of the Thompson's gazelle was to hide in the grass while the mother kept her distance so as not to attract predators. I had to be careful when driving the veldt at night not to run over the babies. So complete was their instinct to hide that they would allow me to approach and lift a tail to determine their sex.

I bottle fed orphans, helped catch animals for veterinary procedures, and had to climb a fence to escape an angry Ankole bull. But one hoofed animal that I never went in with was the Cape buffalo. They lived in their own separate, moated exhibit. That was probably because these fierce, bovine animals stand about five feet tall at the shoulder and weigh more than a thousand pounds. It is said that they can fight off a pride of lions when threatened and will lie in wait to ambush and kill big-game hunters when wounded.

Our male Cape buffalo, after I let him out of his night house one morning and closed the massive steel sliding door, turned around and hit the door with such force, he sent it swinging up on its overhead track. The bottom track which had been anchored in the concrete, came flying into the middle of the room. Once he had made his point, he walked calmly out to munch on the pile of hay I had left in his enclosure.

I was comfortable around all types of animals so, when the Toronto Zoo asked me to escort a shipload of hoofed animals from Europe, I jumped at the chance.

People have been capturing wild animals and bringing them into captivity for as long as we have had the capacity to do so. It seems that there is something in our nature that causes us to be fascinated by rare and unusual creatures. Part of the plunder of early explorers was a selection of the rare and beautiful creatures that inhabited far-off lands.

The Dutch East India Company, for example, was a major supplier of animals to Europe in the seventeenth and eighteenth centuries. The company even constructed special pens and stables in the port of

Rotterdam, where an Indian rhino named Clara arrived from India in July 1741.

While large companies like the Dutch East India Company had most of the business of importing animals, some creatures, like the giraffe that arrived at Marseille, France, in October 1826, arrived in Europe through individual shippers.

When Zarafa arrived in Marseilles she astonished audiences. After wintering in the south of France to rest and acclimate to her new surroundings, she set out on foot for Paris in May 1827. It was reported that over 100,000 people came to see her—approximately an eighth of the population of Paris at the time. Zarafa was an ambassador from an exotic land, and she captivated the French people for many years. She lived out her life as part of the royal menagerie until her death in 1845.

Transporting animals by ship is a time-honored tradition—a tradition that I experienced firsthand. If people could successfully ship a rhinoceros ten thousand miles from India to Northern Europe or a giraffe across the Mediterranean with its head protruding through the deck of the ship, how difficult could it be to transport a half-dozen camels, a couple of tigers, and some hoofed animals across the Atlantic—especially on a modern, twentieth-century freighter?

One of the more exhilarating experiences of my life was standing on the deck of the Polish freighter

Lessons from the Zoo

Zawiercie at the docks of Bremerhaven, Germany, on the afternoon of June 8, 1974. Located in northwestern Germany on an estuary that runs directly into the North Sea, the port of Bremerhaven is one of the largest container ports in the world and was, as I recall, a major operation in those days as well. The *Zawiercie* would be my home for the next two weeks as we chugged across the North Atlantic en route to the port of Montreal. I may have been retracing the route of the *Titanic*, but this was no pleasure cruise. I received cursory instructions on how to care for my cargo of twenty animals that were being loaded onto the deck and secured under my watchful, though inexperienced, eye.

As a trained zookeeper working for the new Metro Toronto Zoo, I was no stranger to the ins and outs of cleaning cages and feeding animals. But animals in crates on the deck of a ship on the open ocean were another matter. What had I gotten myself into?

Stocking a major zoo with the thousands of animals needed to fill the exhibits meant hundreds of shipments arriving in Toronto from all over the world. Animals from North America could arrive by truck, while smaller animals from overseas could fly into Toronto's international airport. But the larger animals from Europe and Asia needed to be transported by ocean-going freighters. It was an age-old method of transport and one that required a caretaker for the long voyage. That is where I came in.

J. D. Porter

On the morning of Saturday, June 8, I boarded the ship, moved into my small room with a bed that would prove way too short for my 6'8" frame, and observed the loading process. By 4:30 p.m., my consignment of twenty animals had been loaded:

1.1 Siberian tigers
1.1 Sarus cranes
0.6 Bactrian camels
0.2 wisent
1.2 yak
1.1 gaur
1.2 red buffalo   (Note: the numbers separated by periods refer to males & females)

Most of the animals occupied crates that were lashed securely to the deck near the rear of the ship. The camels, however, were not in crates. They were in pens that had been constructed on each side of the central hatch opening, three animals to a pen. The man who had delivered the animals to the dock gave me hurried instructions in broken English that covered cleaning and feeding.

In the morning, I was to clean all crates and cages, provide water for all animals, and feed hay and grain to the camels and hoofed stock. In the afternoon, my schedule called for another round of cleaning all crates and cages followed by feeding hay. The six camels received two bales of hay each day for all animals with very little grain. The hoofed animals received varying amounts of hay and grain. I offered the sarus cranes some bird pellets along with some finely chopped lettuce or apple. I had meat for the tigers, which I fed every three days.

On Sunday morning, June 9, we were still tied up at the dock, and I already had my first casualty. One of the sarus cranes was lying down in its crate and was dead by 4 p.m. I fed the rest of the animals but was unable to clean their crates because of the workers on the deck. The camels caused me another worry because they were in pens, not in crates, and I was not sure how I would manage their feeding and cleaning routines. I was also worried about their humps.

The Bactrian camel is the two-humped variety that is native to Central Asia. Their fatty humps are taller and thinner than the single hump of the dromedary, so they tend to flop a bit and can even lie over the camel's side. Before I boarded the ship, my travels in Europe had included a stop in Gelsenkirchen, Germany, at the small zoo and holding compound where the camels were being held. When I arrived, I was handed a telegram from Gunter Voss, director of the Toronto, Zoo. It read:

Camels for Toronto must have standing humps as per agreement with importer. Therefore, inspect carefully. You are entitled to reject unsatisfactory specimens. If in doubt, telephone Mr. Cahill or me. Greetings, Voss.

The owner of the Gelsenkirchen Zoo, Hermann Ruhe, was a third-generation animal supplier. His grandfather had begun supplying animals to zoos and circuses in the 1880s. I was a twenty-five-year-old zookeeper who was on a wide-eyed tour of Europe. The possibility of a confrontation with the legendary animal dealer over my opinion of camel humps was disconcerting, to say the least. Some humps were leaning a bit, but I wasn't about to reject any of them. Now, on board the ship, I wasn't so sure I had made the right decision!

The wooden crates that held the hoofed animals had lift-up sliding doors at the front and back ends. Each door had two nails side by side, one in the door and one in the crate, with a one-foot-long piece of wire tied to each nail. This allowed the doors to slide open about a foot for feeding at the front end and raking out manure at the other. The wire would, hopefully, prevent the animal from hooking a horn or a hoof under the door and sliding it open.

I considered Monday, June 10, to be the beginning of the journey, even though we had been on board since Saturday, because this was when we set sail at 6:30 p.m. We were finally on our way, cruising through the North Sea and into the English Channel.

The day had not been without its drama, however. It turned out we were going to make an unscheduled stop in Rouen, France, and because of quarantine restrictions and our animal health certificates, we had to get permission from the Canadian government to stop there. I also had a visit from a veterinarian from Bremen to check the dead crane. After a cursory look at the animal, he said to throw it overboard when we were out at sea.

Day 2 (*Journal Entries*)

A bit of rough, damp weather this a.m. put the animals (including me) off feed & water. Weather calmed into a beautiful sunny afternoon & all animals got grain mix except little buffalo would not eat or drink. This animal "moos" a lot & doesn't eat well. I think it is too young for a journey like this and, if any animal doesn't make it, it will probably be this one. Gaur have the shits, so I cut back hay a little but still fed some grain. Camels were shaky this a.m. They are OK in rough seas because they lie down, but they can't or won't drink like this. Could be a problem. Wisent seem always to be hungry.

Day 3

I worked hard this morning, cleaning and feeding so I could enjoy our cruise up the Seine River. It was six and a half hours from the coast to Rouen, France, where I spent the evening walking around the City looking at cathedrals.

Day 4

A French veterinarian checked the animals and we left Rouen at 10:30 p.m. – finally headed for Canada.

Day 5

A beautiful sunny day with a chilly north wind, but otherwise weather was perfect. All the animals are in good shape. Spent their seventh day in crates on the ship and, except for fecal material sticking to their fur, they all seemed fine. Shipboard life is very dull. We eat at eight, twelve, three, and five thirty. In between, I do the animals, and read and write. There is only one group of English-speaking people on board. Everyone else speaks German or Polish. Then there's my friend Mr. Krinkle, a German World War Two POW who speaks some English.

Day 6

A cold north wind continued today, stirring up some choppy water. I was seasick in the morning and returned to bed after feeding grain. I took a two-hour nap, skipped lunch, and felt better this afternoon. I finished cleaning and feeding and watering. Smooth sailing this evening. Cloudy tonight hope it doesn't rain tomorrow.

Day 7

Sunday, June 16th–Happy Father's Day.

A cloudy, windy cold day in the north Atlantic. Choppy water makes going rough but not sick today. The two yaks and the young Congo buffalo are not eating or drinking well for second day – eating hay, but no grain.

Day 8

Another cloudy dull foggy day we seem always to be heading directly into a stiff wind. Captain says we lose about 1/2 mph. Two female yaks and young Congo buffalo eating hay but not grain. One female wisent still will not eat alfalfa changing her back to regular hay. Male gaur has swollen left rear foot, probably from kicking crate. eating and drinking OK. We are halfway across the Atlantic.

Day 9

Coldest, windiest, cloudiest day of the journey. The ship fights a stiff wind and leans so much I sometimes think we'll turn over. The captain says we'll be just off Newfoundland, Canada tomorrow. Today was the coldest day of the journey. Rough to work in this weather.

Day 10

The wind and fog have finally eased, but it is very cold at about 35° and cloudy. The pace has slowed to a crawl because we are in iceberg territory. We passed near one this morning—the first iceberg I've seen.

Day 11

A lousy way to travel and if you're in a hurry. We are out of the iceberg zone in and into a fog so thick we can't even see the bow of the ship. We were still at a snail's pace when we finally sailed into the sunshine at 2 p.m. We still can't see Canada, even though the map shows we're just off the southern coast of Newfoundland. We finally spotted land at 4 p.m.

Day 12

More fog this morning, but weather it is much warmer. It turned into a nice day. Cleaned all crates and both camel pens much work but this is the last day tomorrow we enter the Saint Lawrence Seaway and take on a pilot. The captain threw me a curve. He says Monday is a holiday and the ship will not be unloaded till Tuesday.

Day 13

A beautiful sunny morning sailing up the Saint Lawrence. Green hills on the north side are beautiful. Took on river pilots at 9 a.m. Captain says we will dock at Montreal tomorrow. Fed and watered all animals today, no more cleaning since we are in the enclosed waterway. Passed Quebec City and the Hotel Frontenac at 7 p.m.—a lovely sight. A beautiful day and beautiful cruise up the Saint Lawrence. A fitting end to a long journey.

Lessons from the Zoo

Day 14–Sunday, June 23rd
For the first time in nearly two weeks, I awoke to a still, silent ship. The engines were shut down sometime during the night when we docked at Montreal.

After a career working with every type of hoofed animal imaginable in conditions that ranged from living free and wild to living in a crate in the middle of the ocean, I thought I had seen it all. But it seems I wasn't finished learning from the animals because there's one in every crowd—even a crowd of mules. I'm talking about that individual who marches to his or her own drummer.

I witnessed such an individual one weekend when our quail hunting lodge hosted the annual meeting of the state chapter of a prominent women's club. The event was a historic preservation tour that brought them to view the plantation home designed by a world-famous architect.

It is worth noting that when quail hunting season ends at the end of February, the animals take the summer off while the property managers are hard at work burning fields, clearing brush, and maintaining equipment. Because it was a private residence and a members-only facility, nobody came on the property unless they had business there. When I arrived that day, the horses and mules were grazing peacefully in their fifty-acre pasture, peacefully that is, until three large white tour busses followed by a small caravan of cars trundled down the dirt road in front of their pasture

I can only imagine what was going through their minds as the vehicles disgorged a hundred or so passengers. Maybe they thought all these people had come to see them—perhaps bringing food. It was quite a sight to see six mules and a dozen horses sprinting across the pasture to gather along the white wooden fence. It reminded me of when I was a kid, and we heard the bells of the ice cream truck jingling through the neighborhood.

The guests, of course, ambled over to the pasture fence to see the animals, but I paid little notice, assuming the people would soon lose interest. Imagine my surprise when I looked back and discovered that the guests had gathered around a mule that was grazing peacefully outside the pasture in the middle of the lawn. How had that happened? Had she jumped the fence? Not likely. Had someone left the gate open? Not according to a quick survey of the fence line.

The mule turned out to be my dependable pulling mule, Thelma. She gave me little trouble as I herded her back up the lane and through a gate that led back to the pasture. She even seemed—if I care to be anthropomorphic—glad to see me.

So how did she get out? Well, that is the interesting bit. According to several guests who witnessed it as they drove in, when the other animals were trotting to the fence, Thelma separated herself and turned ninety degrees from the herd. She proceeded with purpose down the fence line, away from the action. She entered a grove of trees where the sturdy wooden fence becomes a tangle of metal posts and barbed wire—a section of fence that was apparently less than secure. Guests reported that she when she emerged from the trees she was no longer in the pasture. She had found a hole in the fence and decided to join the party.

How, I wonder, did she figure that out? How did she have the presence of mind to zig when the rest of the herd zagged? Thelma was apparently heeding the advice of poet Ralph Waldo Emerson—advice that has been a hallmark of my career as I moved from zoo job to zoo job, and advice that serves as lesson number three: *Do not go where the path may lead, go instead where there is no path, and leave a trail.*

LESSON 4

Do unto Apes

Easily the most intimidating experience in my evening routine as a trainee keeper at Busch Gardens was the trip out to Chimp Island. Our access was across a water moat, which trapped us on an island with a family of chimpanzees that included one of the most menacing animals in the park—a male chimp named Bamboo. The boat was a flat-bottomed aluminum johnboat, which was fastened to a rope that stretched from shore to shore. We pulled ourselves over to a cave-like opening in the rockwork that was protected from the chimps by an elaborate array of electrified wires. Once inside the holding area, Bamboo greeted us every day with his threatening display of foot-stomping, hooting, and screaming, culminating in a shower of poop that he scooped up from the floor in a smooth underhand motion, peppering us with deadly accuracy. The experienced hands knew to duck out of the doorway at the right moment—a knack they always failed to mention to the new guy. But what made Bamboo even more frightening was his reputation.

Two years before I became a zookeeper at the Gardens, according to news reports, a thirty-four-year-old animal attendant named Angelo Morales was attacked by Bamboo when he went across the moat for the morning feeding. After feed was placed and animals were shifted, one of the cages had been accidentally left unlocked. The one-hundred-thirty-pound, six-year-old chimp attacked and bit Morales on the back of his left leg. The report said Morales was admitted to the hospital and was left with a deep gash on his leg. But when I met Angelo a few years after the incident, his scar was much more than a deep gash. It looked like Bamboo had removed most of the calf muscle. To see Angelo limping around the commissary preparing animal diets was a constant reminder of the dangers inherent in the profession.

A few years after I left Busch Gardens, I found myself caring for another ape. This one was a thirty-pound male baby gorilla named Joseph that arrived at the Metro Toronto Zoo on the evening of May 9, 1974. My partner and I had just returned to the zoo late one evening from the airport. Our job had been to pick up two wooden crates from an international flight, return to the zoo, and uncrate the animals. We were to give them some food and water and, if they appeared healthy, leave them for the night. The veterinarians would give them a thorough exam in the morning.

While my partner was down the hall tending to his own crate, I sat cross-legged in a twelve-foot-by-twelve-foot holding stall in the zoo's quarantine building. The heavy bedding of wood shavings and straw was both comfortable to sit in and soothing in its scent of fresh pine. I lifted the crate's sliding door out of its track, laid it on top of the wooden crate, and settled a few feet from the opening, peering into the darkness of the small box. My plan was to sit quietly and wait for the baby gorilla to emerge.

We sat staring at each other for a long time. He had settled with his back toward the far end of the crate, glancing at me without making direct eye contact. He was thirty pounds of black fur and dark eyes, clearly frightened, and unsure of what to do next. As I was about to give up and leave him to explore his new surroundings after I left, he stirred and walked calmly out of the crate and into my lap. He smelled earthy—a combination of freshly turned soil and over-ripe fruit.

I wanted to comfort the little guy and welcome him to his new home. I knew he would be safe and well cared for, with the best food, other gorillas for companionship, and modern veterinary care. It would be some time before I learned the real story of how baby gorillas came to be at the zoo. For now,

I just wrapped my arms around him as I would one of my own sons.

The label on his crate hinted at the story of his journey. He had been shipped from Nairobi, Kenya, by an Austrian animal dealer named Heini Demmer. Joseph and his mate down the hall, Josephine, had been captured in the wild. But I had no idea how he came to be in Canada, sitting in my lap. I would later learn that it was a tragic story—probably similar to that of a young chimpanzee I came to know a few years later.

A few years before Joseph was shipped out of Nairobi, Kenya, another infant ape was captured four-thousand miles to the west in Liberia. Chimpanzee families do not easily give up their young, so he probably watched all the chimps around him be killed by humans—hunters who would have utilized the adults for the bushmeat trade and sold the babies as pets.

In December 1966, an American named Ed Schultz was working for an iron-ore mining company in the west African port of Buchanan, Liberia. When he heard that someone at the mess hall was selling that baby chimp, Schultz knew the animal would be much better off in his home than some of the alternatives. He found the man, bought the chimp for a few dollars in cash, and took him home to meet his wife and children. The Schultzes named him Herman. They fed him from a baby bottle, put him in diapers, and taught him to eat his fruit and drink from a cup at the dinner table. A few months later, a female they named Gitta, joined Herman in the Schultz household.

Herman and Gitta were raised as part of the Schultz family and came to the United States when the family returned home. When Mr. Schultz found himself working for a phosphate company near Tampa, Florida, Herman and Gitta were about five years old. They had grown to a size that meant they would soon be too strong to handle. Given the unpredictable nature of adolescent chimps, they could pose a danger.

By 1971, Schultz was looking for a new home for Herman and Gitta and decided to donate them to Lowry Park Zoo. In those days, the zoo was run by the City of Tampa and was a stark and perhaps even grim place. But, to Ed, Lowry Park seemed like the best choice for his chimps. The zoo was ready to give Herman and Gitta a cage that was larger than the one they were kept in with the Schultzes.

On June 10, 1971, a *Tampa Tribune* photographer captured Mayor Dick Greco with the Lowry Park Zoo's new chimps visiting his office. The following year, in June 1972, Herman and I were featured in the *St. Petersburg Times* newspaper article. He was just a little guy—about six years old. A photo of him in the article evokes a sense of despair even though he appears relaxed with one foot propped up on the bars as he picks intently at a piece of fruit. He had only been in those cramped, dank quarters for about a year, but the real tragedy was that he would live there for another dozen years before our paths would cross again and I would be privileged to do something about his condition.

In the spring of 1984, twelve years after my entry into the zoo business, the City of Tampa Parks Department hired me as director of the municipal zoo. I had left Toronto in 1978 to become the general curator of the Louisville Zoo and being the director of a zoo was my dream job. Unfortunately, my career advancement had come at a price. My marriage had fallen apart, largely as a result of my selfish focus on animal care and hours spent at the pub after work. I spent more time with the animals at the zoo than I did with my family. Tampa was a new beginning, both professionally and personally. In the summer of 1984, I married the love of my life. By this time, I had developed plenty of compassion for the animals, but still had work to do in my personal life.

The Lowry Park Zoo was quite a letdown for me in many ways, after having worked at modern zoos in Toronto and Louisville. The cages I inherited were mostly chain-link boxes of various sizes that housed lions, tigers, pumas, jaguars, bears, and primates. The two chimpanzees, Herman and Gitta, lived behind iron bars covered with heavy chain-link fencing that rendered them almost invisible, while otters and alligators floated in water-filled pits. The lone elephant, Shena, was confined to a small pen with a shelter about the size of a two-car garage.

It was a free zoo, which might explain why it was necessary to post crude wooden signs on most cages that warned: *City Code: cruelty to or harassment of animals is prohibited & subject to imprisonment & fine.* But the good news was that all of that was about to change. The Lowry Park Zoo Association had been formed in 1982, at the suggestion of the Tampa Parks Department, to raise awareness of the zoo and to promote a public-private partnership that would fund its renaissance.

When we announced the rebirth of the zoo in the summer of 1984, we heard from plenty of naysayers. They questioned the need for another zoo when we already had Busch Gardens. They scoffed at the idea of paying admission to a city zoo. And they really took exception to the multimillion-dollar price tag attached to the venture—a price that seemed to be escalating. But as the plans were unveiled, minds began to change. Mayor Bob Martinez had a vision that was shared by the Lowry Park Zoo Association, a group that was led by Lowry family member Sally Lowry Baldwin.

We revealed the design plans for the new zoo a few weeks after my arrival and Mayor Bob Martinez committed $5 million of city money to get the project started in phase one. A month after that, the Lowry Park Zoo Association announced it was moving ahead with its fundraising efforts in order to finance the first phase of the zoo renovation.

We held our first event in August 1984 when we unveiled a master plan. Our design would use water barriers and dry moats to create naturalistic habitats for the animals while increasing the size of the zoo from eleven acres to twenty-four acres. The city of Tampa offered a million dollars to fund the initial site preparation and infrastructure improvements. This was in addition to its $5 million pledge for phase one of the zoo's development. With the city firmly committed, the Zoo Association expanded its vision and embarked on a $20 million capital campaign. The project would include an Asian Domain (with elephants, tigers, bears, tapirs, and camels), a World of Primates, and an aviary. The plan was being developed by a New Orleans based firm, Design Consortium.

Momentum built and we went from one of our first donations in June 1984, of just over two hundred dollars from the Boys and Girls Club of Tampa, to regular six-figure donations. We raised millions of dollars in a few short years.

It was the perfect public/private partnership. We had a popular mayor and his enlightened administration working with the community's "movers and shakers." As the construction began to show impressive progress, the excitement grew—and donors lined up. In 1987 alone, we received $500,000 from the Jim Walter Corporation for the World of Primates, $500,000 from Barnett Bank of Tampa for the aviary, and $100,000 from CitiCorp for the sloth bear exhibit. By this time, nearly $10 million had been raised privately and the city of Tampa had increased its funding to $8 million.

This was not a simple renovation project or the construction of some new exhibits. The entire zoo was being demolished and a new zoo built in its place. But where could we put the animals? We decided to stockpile them in an unused area of the park and utilize existing cages to house them.

In March 1985, we closed the zoo to the public and began relocating the animals. One advantage to having animals in such primitive conditions was that their new temporary facilities could hardly be worse, and in some cases, the temporary cages were an improvement.

We installed concrete slabs with drainage, sidewalks, and other infrastructure. After shifting the animals into holding areas, we cut the cages from their floors, picked them up with a giant crane, swung them to the new location, and welded them to their floor in the new location. Animals were transferred into new cages in a new location out of the way of construction.

I met Ed Schultz soon after I arrived as director of the zoo in 1984, and he was pleased that our master plan would provide Herman and Gitta a spacious grassy area in the World of Primates. But first, they would need to move out of the way of construction. A new, temporary cage was assembled a few hundred yards from their old home and in the summer of 1985, we tranquilized the chimps and moved them. Their new space was a big improvement over the old, oppressive cage. The old exhibit was a block building with a fifteen- by twenty-foot exhibit space. Visitors viewed the chimps through a double layer of chain-link attached inside and outside of the structure's iron bars, making it nearly impossible to see the animals. The new cage—though only temporary—was more spacious, and it was open on all sides, instead of being backed-up to a building. It wasn't an ideal situation, but it was a slight improvement, and in a few years, things would get even better.

By late 1985, all the zoo cages had been moved and all the animals transferred. It was time for the serious construction to begin. An army of workers dug cavernous holes, poured massive concrete footings, and the outline of a new zoo began to take shape. The first phase would be built around three themes—an Asian Domain, a walk-through aviary, and a World of Primates that would be the new home for the chimps. The public areas would consist of new ticketing, entry, and gift shop. An impressive central plaza would feature a fountain around a pair of bronze manatees. For nearly three years, workers poured concrete, sculpted artificial rocks, and installed caging. Primatologist, Jane Goodall paid the chimps a visit in 1987, and by the end of that year, we were planting grass, testing waterfalls, and moving animals into their new homes.

The new chimpanzee area was not especially large, but it was an interesting and varied space for animals that had only known concrete and chain-link. Large logs and an artificial termite mound broke up a long, grassy yard. A deep dry moat afforded the chimps an unobstructed view of their human visitors and the landscape beyond. One of the highlights of my zoo career came in the winter of 1988 when I witnessed Herman and Gitta step out of their new night house and walk on grass for the first time in many years. Herman climbed atop what would become his favorite perch—the termite mound—to gaze back at me. I am not suggesting that he was actually "happy," but I do know that I did everything in my power to make him so and would continue to try to improve the lives of the animals under my care for the rest of my career.

Five years later, for example, one of my first projects as Deputy Director of the Toledo Zoo was the $3 million Kingdom of the Apes area that opened in 1993. Toledo had an impressive collection of great apes that included chimpanzees, orangutans, and two families of gorillas. They lived in a symmetrical, rectangular, 1970s–era facility, with each of the four groups housed in a section that consisted of off-exhibit holding cages, a small indoor glass-fronted dayroom, and a slightly larger open-air outdoor space with a concrete floor. It was all hard-scape—concrete, glass, and steel. No animals had access to grass.

The renovation would improve the holding cages and add an eighteen-thousand-square-foot outdoor gorilla meadow and a three-story indoor dayroom. The old outdoor spaces would have a tall cage structure added to increase the vertical space, and grass would be planted to replace the concrete floor. It was a remarkable transformation, both visually and for the quality of life of the animals.

On Monday, May 17, 1993, I gathered with my colleagues to watch the male gorilla Akbar peer out of the holding area and carefully test the grassy surface of the new Gorilla Meadow exhibit. As soon as he determined it was safe, he allowed females Happy, Malaika, and Elaine to follow. The thrill of seeing the gorillas step into the sunshine was tempered by the concern we felt as Akbar carefully inspected the walls and fences of his new home. Only after he completed his tour of the perimeter and did not find any escape routes did we relax and celebrate our success.

When Joseph, the baby gorilla emerged from his crate in 1974, he sat on my lap for a few seconds, facing away from me. Without warning, he placed his mouth over my bare right forearm, and, in slow motion, he bit down—hard. So hard, in fact, that I hollered in pain and jerked my arm away. I pushed him out of my lap as gently as I could under the painful circumstances and left the pen to examine my injury. The bite broke the skin slightly, leaving a bloody imprint of his upper and lower teeth like some dental impression. My worries about what diseases he might be carrying escalated ten days later when he died. As it turned out, he had no transmissible diseases, and obviously, I have survived with no ill effects. Fortunately, this was long before we knew about the Ebola virus and the other deadly diseases coming out of Africa, or I would have been well and truly frightened! Joseph died on May 20 of what was thought to be a nutritional deficiency.

Mankind's history of dealing with our nearest ancestors is shameful. We have subjected them to terrifying methods of capture, harrowing journeys to foreign lands, and years of cruel confinement. One well-known example was Ivan the gorilla. He was captured in the early 1960s as an infant in the Congo and lived for more than twenty years in a cage in a Tacoma Washington department store until 1994 when he was sent to live in Zoo Atlanta's Ford African Rainforest. He spent his last twenty years rolling in the grass and cavorting with other gorillas.

I have seen many changes in the time I have been in the zoo business, but none are as dramatic as the change in philosophy on how we interact with the apes. We no longer accept them from the wild, we have them live in large family groups, and we teach them to voluntarily submit to regular health exams.

Ape habitats at modern zoos are a close approximation to the homes they would have in the wild—without the threat of being killed by poachers. Anyone who works with apes, as I have, can't help but appreciate how closely we are related and how important it is that we treat them with compassion.

When I was growing up, I was taught something called the "Golden Rule." Later, I came to learn it was based on a passage from the Bible—a passage that applies to how we should treat other people and, I believe, the animals that share our planet. Lesson number four comes from Matthew 7:12: *So in everything, do to others what you would have them do to you.*

LESSON 5

A Fear of Snakes

My brother Danny tells the story of receiving a terrifying surprise while walking home from baseball practice one summer afternoon when he was young. He was taking a shortcut through the woods behind our house in a rural part of St. Petersburg, Florida. The gulf coast of Florida in the 1960s was not the thriving metropolis it is today. St. Petersburg was a sleepy retirement village that was carpeted with miles of woodlands and abundant wildlife—including plenty of snakes.

In the woods around our house, we had nonvenomous snakes like garter snakes and water snakes; red bellies and red necks; hognose, racers, and coachwhips; pine snakes, rat snakes, and king snakes. We also had plenty of venomous snakes, including coral snakes, water moccasins, pygmy rattlers, and—the granddaddy of them all—the Eastern diamondback rattlesnake. We knew that the Eastern diamondback could grow to nearly six feet in length and be as big around as a man's forearm. Its broad flat head, compact powerful coils, and loud buzzing rattle was the stuff of legend in our neighborhood. According to the *Peterson Field Guide to Reptiles*, the Eastern diamondback is "at home in the palmetto Flatwoods and dry Pinelands of the South." That describes the hundred or so acres of woods behind our house. That was our playground. My brother was in familiar territory.

Danny had to scramble down a deep ravine on his way home that afternoon and toss his baseball glove up the other side so he could climb out of the ditch. But as he pulled himself up, he came face to face with a diamondback rattlesnake curled up and agitated at the glove that had been tossed on the ground next to it. Danny carefully lowered himself back down and circled around to find a new route home. When he and my dad went back to retrieve the glove, the snake was gone.

Snakes were a part of our lives growing up, and we were taught to have a healthy respect for them—especially the ones that could kill us. That did not deter us from using the woods as our playground. On a daily basis, we rode our bikes along dirt roads, chased each other down meandering animal trails, and played hide and seek amongst the dwarf palmetto bushes. The only snake bite I remember was our friend Ricky, who was bitten on the toe by a pygmy rattler. I saw the fang marks on his toe as he stood on the front seat of his father's truck (no seatbelts in those days) while his dad spoke to mine. Nobody seemed to be in a hurry. In later years, my dad allowed a big black snake to live in his tool shed to control the rodents, but when he had four young sons playing in the yard and woods, the only good snake was . . . well, you know.

It seems that the more our parents warned us, the more determined we were to ignore them. It must have sunk in eventually because, as an adult, those activities make me cringe. When I lived in the northern United States, I even had to unlearn the habit of keeping my eyes glued to the ground as I walked through the woods. There were few venomous snakes to worry about in the North. Now that I live in the South again, I have relearned my old habits. When I am working in the garden or taking out the compost, I carefully watch wherever I am about to place my feet or hands. Though I am happy to see snakes in my yard, I still recoil a bit.

When I began my zoo career at Busch Gardens, we didn't have any snakes in our animal collection. But that changed when I moved to the Toronto Zoo. As senior keeper of the North American Pavilion, I had two cages of snakes to care for. One cage had an assortment of nonvenomous North American snakes—rat snakes, garter snakes, and king snakes. The other contained a half-dozen massasauga rattlesnakes. This small species, only growing to a little over two feet in length, had a gray background color with a row of large black blotches or spots down the center of the back. The massasauga is also called the "swamp rattler" because it prefers the wet prairies, bogs, and swamps of the northern United States and southern Ontario in Canada.

Most zoos have specialized zookeepers who care for mammals, birds, and reptiles, but Toronto was trying a new concept. We were expected to be generalists, caring for every species in our section—including rattlesnakes. I learned how to feed them small mice with a pair of tongs and to clean their cage by using a snake hook to transfer them to a garbage can.

As my career advanced and I began doing programs on behalf of the various zoos I represented, snakes became a part of my life. It was the creature that audiences loved to hate. People often got up from their seats and sometimes even left the room. I handled boa constrictors, ball pythons, and rat snakes. I learned not to recoil at the feel of their muscular legless bodies that were wrapped in a smooth, dry leathery skin. I marveled at their forked tongues as they tickled the hairs of my arm, picking up scent molecules to transfer to the "smell" organ inside the roof of their mouth.

I confidently handled snakes and regaled my audiences with their importance to the ecosystem, all the while trying to conceal my fear that one of the snakes might turn and bite me. They were all non-venomous, but the mere thought made the hairs on my arms tingle. I learned to overcome a powerful urge to recoil while I reached into a cloth bag to pull out a creature that terrified me. Though I handled many snakes during my career, I never did work up the courage to handle the venomous ones.

When the movie *Jaws* came out in 1975, I found some new creatures to fear. People seemed to take such delight at being frightened by movie animals, *Jaws* was followed by a movie called *Alligator* in 1980. The realization that I had spent my youth swimming in the shark-filled waters of the Gulf of Mexico and alligator-infested Florida lakes put my fear of snakes into a new perspective. Snakes might bite me, but sharks and alligators could eat me.

To the best of my knowledge, I never had any close calls with sharks or alligators, but I did see plenty of alligators in the wild. At Lake Maggiore in St. Petersburg, I observed huge gators that hauled out onto my uncle's lawn to bask. As children, we swam among the alligators in Lake Tarpon, a lake in Northern Pinellas County. Our splashing must have kept them at bay because we never saw them come near our dock.

When I entered the zoo business, captive alligators and crocodiles became a part of my life. I cared for or managed alligators at the Toronto Zoo and the

Lowry Park Zoo. The Toledo Zoo had an entire building devoted to reptiles, including some crocodiles in a greenhouse section we called the "Crocodile Solarium." When we visited Africa, we sipped cocktails at Samburu Lodge a few feet from basking twelve-foot long Nile crocodiles across a low stone wall.

Most of the crocodilians I dealt with were placid, except at feeding time or if we were trying to catch them. But they are not gentle, placid creatures by nature. Consider the story told by circus man, W. C. Coup in his 1901 book, *Sawdust & Spangles, Stories & Secrets of the Circus*.

When he ran the New York aquarium, Coup received a shipment of forty alligators from Florida and had his men place all the animals in an empty whale tank. The gators ranged in length from one foot to twelve feet. According to Coup's account:

Although the tank was an immense one, these forty reptiles did not have as much room as they would have liked. This overcrowding was doubtless the cause of a most terrible fight between them, which occurred very soon after they were installed in their new quarters. Nearly all the larger "gators" took part in it, springing at each other and locking their jaws with a resounding, crashing noise that could be heard all over the building. While thus locked together, they would toss each other about and swish their tails with such vigor as to destroy the tank,

> *breaking the thick glass. Our attendants were almost paralyzed with fear and confusion at the strange battle and vainly endeavored to separate the combatants. There seemed, however, to be no way of doing this, as they would snap at each other so violently as to break each other's jaws, and this horrible snap really sounded like the report of a gun. To prevent their escape into the exhibition room, a temporary barrier was soon erected until they became exhausted and the battle was over. The tank was made of glass one and one-fourth inches thick, embedded in cement and bound with solid iron columns. It was destroyed in ten minutes.*

Today, we have a better understanding of alligator and crocodile behavior. We would know better than to dump forty gators of various sizes into a big tank. We are also able to do some rudimentary training, which I observed when I was Executive Director of Chehaw Wild Animal Park. We had a large pond that contained more than two dozen alligators of all sizes.

When Chehaw moved from whole prey items like chicken to a prepared pelleted diet, the staff was presented with an opportunity to use this new food as a reward item for training. The objective was to train each animal to come to the edge of the pond and take food from the zookeepers so that food intake could be monitored. The protocol, as I recall, was for the keeper to enter the enclosure and approach the pond. The alligators would swim over for feeding and station themselves at the waterline. By conditioning crocodilians to feed in a regimented manner, zoos can monitor the animal's overall condition, appetite, dental condition, injuries, and total food consumption. This allowed for quicker detection of any potential issues.

The proper term for a fear of snakes is ophidiophobia. It is a common phobia that can be triggered by a variety of factors that sound familiar to me. This could include living in an environment that prominently featured snakes and being taught they were something to fear. It could also stem from a traumatic experience with a snake, like the one my brother relayed to me. Or, as one who was raised a Methodist, it could be my religious training. Everyone in my family knew that the devil himself took the form of a snake in the Garden of Eden.

But my fear of snakes could also be intrinsic—a part of my DNA. Recent research has found that certain neurons in the brain only respond to snakes. These snake-dedicated neurons may be a legacy of our distant primate past since we share this bias toward snakes with monkeys. When primates evolved some sixty-million years ago, they adapted to living in trees, searching for food at night, and sleeping in the canopy during the day. Snakes creeping through those trees were among their deadliest enemies.

Lessons from the Zoo

When I worked at the Toledo Zoo, I was especially thankful to have a team of experts handling the reptiles for me. As deputy director, one of the areas I oversaw was the reptile house. Toledo had an impressive reptile collection, but the most impressive animal of all was Raj, the king cobra.

According to newspaper reports, Raj was captured in the wilds of Thailand in 1990 and was estimated to be about ten years of age. I don't know how one goes about capturing a twelve-foot king cobra in the wild, but a clue might be found in the writings of one of the old-time animal suppliers.

Perhaps the best-known animal supplier in the early years of the twentieth century was Frank Buck. His 1930 book, *Bring 'Em Back Alive*, was a best seller that catapulted him to worldwide fame. His exploits would have been typical of the animal business in those days. He spent months in the wilderness capturing animals, weeks at sea bringing them back to America, and moments of sheer terror when things went wrong. This was long before the advent of tranquilizer darts. It was a time of steady nerves, lucky breaks, and—even allowing for possible embellishments to help sell his books—considerable bravery.

Frank Buck became a household name because of his ability to romanticize the business of capturing wild animals. His stories may have been embellished, but they are still vivid and believable. His account of the capture of a huge python is a good example.

His group happened upon it by chance. When they first saw the snake, Buck wrote, it was in deep grass near a large tree, and his heart came up in his throat when he saw its size. It looked as big around as a sewer pipe and its eyes, small as they were, seemed as big as saucers.

When one of his guides touched the snake's tail with a long stick, Buck said it reared around instantly, thrashing in the grass, and charged at them with its head raised. If we can believe the story, Buck managed to throw a lasso over its head and wrap the rope around a nearby tree. Once the snake was secured, they cut down a long straight sapling and stretched out the python from where its head was lashed to the tree. Buck's men tied the snake's body securely along the sapling with pieces of vine.

Back at camp, they prepared a large packing case and slid the top back a few inches. They stuffed the snake's head into the box and shoved a bit more in as they cut the rest of the bindings, pushing in coil after coil until the whole twenty-eight feet of its length was safely inside the box.

The king cobra is the world's longest venomous snake and is native to India and Southeast Asia. Raj was about twelve feet long, but they can grow to eighteen feet. An aggressive and deadly snake, they have been known to chase people when provoked. An eighteen-foot cobra can rear up about one-third of its body length to look a six-foot man in the eye. I was thankful that Raj was almost never handled. He had an adjacent cage into which he was shifted for feeding and to allow his cage to be safely cleaned.

A herpetologist once told me that he felt that the king cobra is one of the most intelligent of all snakes. Raj, for me, was the stuff of nightmares. Large, deadly, and smart—the trifecta for an ophidiophobe.

During my four decades in the zoo business, I worked at seven zoos in six different cities. I moved from Florida to Canada, eventually back to Florida, then to South Dakota and Toledo, before finding my way to South Georgia. All my moves were voluntary and resulted in career advancement, but as I look back on my odyssey, I wonder what compelled me to move so often. Some people fear change and would be reluctant to move across the country. I was, it appears, more afraid of staying in one place.

Lesson number five comes from my dealings with reptiles and was best stated by Franklin D. Roosevelt, who said in his 1933 inaugural address: *Let me assert my firm belief that the only thing we have to fear is fear itself—nameless, unreasoning, unjustified terror which paralyzes needed efforts to convert retreat into advance.*

I am not fearful of many things. I am not afraid of the dark. I am not afraid of flying. I am not afraid of spiders. I am not afraid of heights. (Actually, that's a lie.) I managed to conquer some of my fears, like the fear of snakes, but moving from zoo job to zoo job stayed with me until my career ended. British philosopher Bertrand Russell said, "To conquer fear is the beginning of wisdom." I have tried to conquer it and become wise but fear, I have come to understand, is a powerful motivator. It can be deep-seated and unreasonable, except when it was motivating me to get out of the way of a charging rhinoceros.

LESSON 6

Never Too Old to Learn

Fear can be a good thing. It can save your life if you respond the right way. It was fear that motivated me to leap out of the way of a pair of charging rhinos. At least that's the way I like to tell the story.

My encounter occurred late one evening at Busch Gardens in the fall of 1971 when my partner and I were moving animals in for the night. I was inside the runway to the white rhino holding barn, removing an obstruction, when my partner carelessly opened the gate to allow the animals to enter the narrow chute that led to their night house. My heart thudded into my throat when I heard a snort and turned to find both animals standing behind me in single file, seeming to wonder what I was doing in their space. I was out of there in a single, spectacular leap. If that had been the black rhinos, they would not have hesitated to spear me with their horns as they trampled me into the Florida sand.

When I began in the zoo business at Busch Gardens, we had both species of African rhinoceros, the black rhino and the white rhino. Their moat-bounded exhibits were located along the track of the monorail, but their holding areas were situated differently. The black rhino holding area was adjacent to the exhibit behind an artificial rock wall. The white rhinos needed to travel down a long runway to access their night house. The runway had gates at each end that consisted of four-inch pipes that slid across the opening. One of those pipes had become lodged in place, and I was inside the chute trying to free it when the rhinos encountered me blocking their access to food.

Rhinos have a keen sense of smell and acute hearing. Both African rhinos have two horns and poor eyesight, which may explain why they will sometimes charge for no reason. Fortunately for me, though the white rhino is the larger of the two species, it lives in herds and is much more docile. Its name is thought to be derived its name from the Dutch word "*weit*," meaning wide. This refers to its mouth, which adapted to cropping the grasses of the open savannah. It is gray, with a long, angular face and a hump on its neck.

The black, or hooked-lipped, rhino has a thick, hairless gray hide and is a solitary browser. Its triangular-shaped upper lip, which ends in a grasping point, is used to eat a large variety of vegetation—including leaves; buds; and shoots of plants, bushes, and trees. It can be found in various habitats that have dense, woody vegetation.

Rhinos, which are found in the tropical climates of Africa and Southeast Asia, have been known and celebrated outside their native lands for hundreds of years. One of the world's most celebrated works of art is Dürer's Rhinoceros—the name commonly given to a woodcut executed by German painter and printmaker Albrecht Dürer in 1515. Dürer was the most famous artist of his day, primarily because of his ability to make his work available to the masses. The new technology of woodcut printing allowed him to mass-produce thousands of copies of the rhino print in his lifetime. Dürer, however, never actually saw a live rhino.

The rhino that inspired Dürer's print was given by an Indian sultan to the king of Portugal in 1515. The Indian rhino was the first to arrive in Europe since the days of the Roman Empire and caused a sensation. Despite its anatomical inaccuracies, Dürer's woodcut became immensely popular in Europe and was copied many times in the following three centuries. It was regarded by Westerners as a true representation of a rhinoceros into the late eighteenth century. Eventually, it was supplanted by more realistic drawings and paintings, particularly those of another Indian rhino named Clara that toured Europe in the 1740s and 1750s. Her travels were documented by Glynis Ridley in her 2004 book, *Clara's Grand Tour*.

Clara was orphaned as an infant but raised in elegant surroundings in a well-to-do household in India. By the age of eight, she had sailed more than ten thousand miles from Calcutta to Rotterdam and had begun her tour of Europe. Her mother had been killed by hunters when Clara was a few months old. She was rescued by the director of the Dutch East India Company and allowed to live inside his home like a family dog until she became too large to handle. She remained imprinted on her human companions, which probably helped her survive the long journey.

The details of her travels around Europe are not clear, but her owner, Douwemout Van der Meer, fashioned some type of heavy-duty carriage for transportation and struck out, allowing people to see the animal for a fee. He and Clara spent time in Vienna, Hannover, Berlin, Frankfurt, Zurich, and countless other cities, towns, and hamlets across Europe where Clara was displayed in town squares, public fairs, and private palaces.

Frequent public weighing and measuring added to a spectacle that would have made P. T. Barnum proud. She traveled by barge down the Rhine River. She visited Versailles, France, where she met King

Lessons from the Zoo

Louis XV and temporarily joined the royal menagerie. Van der Meer kept her alive and on the road for an astonishing seventeen-year grand tour of Europe, where she amazed and delighted her admirers until she died in London in April 1758.

Today, rhinos are common in zoo collections but are endangered in the wild. When I began working with black rhinos in the 1970s, there were an estimated fifty-thousand animals in the wild. Today, that number has dropped a staggering 90 percent to around five thousand. The reason—poaching. Their horn, it seems, is more valuable on the black market than either gold or cocaine.

My first day on the job at the Toledo Zoo was August 9, 1991. The day before I began, a female white rhino named Bernadine fell from a ledge in her exhibit. We speculated that she had been lying next to a rock outcrop and simply rolled off—like a person might roll out of bed in the middle of the night. The white rhino has a hump on the back of its neck. When she landed on that hump, I suspect the impact fractured a vertebra in her neck. Bernadine was paralyzed and unable to move. Her exhibit had opened a few years earlier and was the result of new concepts in zoo design. Was that complex design a contributing factor?

In the 1980s, while I was helping design and construct a modern zoo with naturalistic exhibits for the City of Tampa, other zoos were making even more improvements. A new concept called landscape immersion was emerging. For several years, zoos had been creating environments in which the animals were provided a space that simulated their natural habitat in the wild. Landscape immersion took that idea a step further. Buildings and barriers were hidden, and the visitor was immersed in the landscape and substrates of the animal areas. Seattle's Woodland Park Zoo won an exhibit award in 1981 for its African Savanna and New Orleans's Audubon Zoo won in 1985 for its Louisiana Swamp. As immersion exhibits began to win accolades and awards, many zoos were forced to recognize their deficiencies.

In 1984, an article in *Parade* magazine labeled the Atlanta Zoo as one of the top ten worst in the nation. The zoo lost its accreditation and outraged residents demanded that the facility be fixed up or closed. Mayor Andrew Young assembled a new management team and privatized the governance of the zoo.

By 1986, the zoo was being redeveloped as Zoo Atlanta and its most ambitious project, the Ford African Rain Forest, opened in 1988. This great ape complex created a lush immersive environment in four naturalistic habitats that were separated by hidden moats. This allowed up to four separate troops of gorillas to interact with each other while visitors could see more than a dozen animals at one time. Specially designed holding areas allowed troops to rotated among the habitats daily.

Lessons from the Zoo

As Zoo Atlanta was being reborn, New York's Bronx Zoo was winning an exhibit award for its new Jungle World. This extraordinary facility was one of the largest and most complex zoo buildings in the world. It captured an acre of land under a roof that rose more than fifty feet into the air. An elevated boardwalk meandered through a space that immersed visitors in the jungle—a space where they were surrounded by hundreds of tropical animals, separated from the public and each other by a series of ravines, streams, and simulated rock outcroppings.

I suppose the size and scope of Jungle World is the reason the Toledo Zoo's groundbreaking exhibit that opened on September 6, 1986, was passed over for an award. Known as the Hippoquarium, the exhibit would allow the Toledo Zoo to boast for decades that it had the world's only 360,000-gallon, filtered pool with underwater viewing for the hippopotamus.

Hippos have been kept in captivity for hundreds of years. There are even accounts of circuses carting hippos around the country in specially designed, water-filled wagons. The problem with exhibiting hippos, however, is that these two-ton animals eat prodigious amounts of vegetation and produce about fifty pounds of waste per day—primarily in the water.

As tempting as it was for zoos to exhibit hippos in their underwater world, the view for the public would resemble a murky mudhole. The Toledo Zoo was first to overcome that obstacle with a state-of-the-art filtration system that pulled water and waste from the pool, screened it to remove the large pieces, and ran the water through sand filters that were similar to but much larger than a residential swimming pool. The final treatment was with ozone, which was a safer and more effective disinfectant for animals than chlorine. The result was a stunning, crystal-clear underwater view of hippos.

As visitors left the hippo viewing area, they became immersed in a simulated African experience called the African Savanna. The Toledo Zoo's African Savanna, which opened in phases from 1987 until 1989, was featured in national publications and hailed as one of the finest zoo experiences in the country. People meandered down winding pathways through a variety of habitats including a Riverine area (with hippos and otters) and the Grassland (with the giraffe, elephant, lion, and meerkat). The white rhinos, Phil and Bernadine, had lived in the grassland area for several years before Bernadine had her accident. The space was relatively small so designers made it seem larger by providing terraces for the animals—terraces that may have led to Bernadine's demise.

Bernadine was too massive to X-ray and too heavy to manipulate for therapy. Staff and volunteers signed up for a round-the-clock vigil. A weeklong effort to save her, including the use of tractors to move her and cranes to lift her, was unsuccessful. As she lay helplessly on her side where she fell, the community response was phenomenal. Construction companies donated equipment, and their operators worked through the night. Concerned citizens flooded us with calls and cards while veterinarians worked feverishly to save her. Unfortunately, Bernadine died shortly after noon on Tuesday, August 13, 1991.

The black rhinos at Busch Gardens frightened me as a young zookeeper. They were flighty, unpredictable, and always took an aggressive approach to any situation. It was charge first and ask questions later—three thousand pounds of meanness and aggression. Any veterinary procedures required a tranquilizer dart, and it seemed to me that even then, things never seemed to go well.

When we received two black rhinos at Chehaw Wild Animal Park in 2006, I expected we might be in for some rough times. Dubya and Sam Houston were a couple of adult males that came from a breeding ranch in Texas and were semi-wild. The first time we locked one of them in our squeeze chute, he went crazy, banging the bars so hard we thought he would either kill himself or break out of the cage and kill us.

But animal care professionals had learned much about animal behavior in the previous few decades. When I was deputy director at the Toledo Zoo in the

1990s, for example, we brought in trainers to help us work with the animals in our collection. These were the people who had learned to train everything from killer whales to parrots. They were confident that their use of something called operant conditioning—using food rewards to elicit a behavior—would work with other species. They were spectacularly successful, and the animal business was transformed. The keepers at Chehaw decided to try operant conditioning on our new rhinos.

After several tedious months of convincing the rhinos that we meant them no harm, they learned to do just about anything for a piece of sweet potato. They would place their noses on the outstretched hand of a keeper when commanded to "target." They stood calmly while staff rubbed them or checked inside their ears. They tolerated groups of rowdy schoolchildren entering their night house. And, most remarkably, I watched a rhino stand still enough to allow a veterinarian to stick a needle into an ankle to draw a blood sample while it calmly took another piece of sweet potato from its keeper.

Thanks to some patience and many hours of training and building trust, these animals went from frightened and insecure to comfortable and docile. Their quality of life improved immensely as they settled into a life of routine activities punctuated by enough changes to make life interesting. The zoo business has evolved during my career and it excites me to imagine how it might change in the next forty or fifty years.

When Dubya and Sam Houston arrived at Chehaw, they were adults and, by some measures, too old to learn "new tricks." But even Shakespeare recognized the fallacy of that when he said, "an unlessoned girl, unschooled, unpracticed; happy in this, she is not yet so old but she may learn." The animals have not changed. We have. We are still learning, but we have much left to discover.

There is an old saying that you can't teach an old dog new tricks. That is simply not true. The rhinos have taught me just the opposite. Lesson six is that we are never too old to learn.

As for me, I am still learning, too. I earned a master's degree from the University of Georgia at the age of sixty, I self-published a novel at sixty-three, learned to drive a mule wagon and wrote a book about it at sixty-six, and I am writing this at seventy. As the celebrated Spanish author Miguel de Cervantes wrote in his classic work *Don Quixote* in the early 1600s: "It's good to live and learn."

LESSON 7

Adapting to Change

The call came into my home just after dinner on Easter Sunday, April 7, 1985. An excited security guard at the Lowry Park Zoo said we had a bear on the loose. As director of the zoo, it fell to me to respond. Karen and I jumped in the car and rushed to the zoo as fast as legally possible, hoping the guard was mistaking a neighborhood dog for one of our two adult black bears. When we arrived, we saw that he was not.

The zoo was undergoing extensive renovation and had been closed to the public a few weeks earlier. But the black bear cages were adjacent to the perimeter fence and still accessible. We had two bears. A three-legged male named, appropriately enough,

Pokey and a female named Ladybug. They inhabited separate cages, but they were placid, docile creatures that were well-accustomed to captivity. On the other hand, bears can be dangerous when provoked. Imagine the fury of an angry, two-hundred-pound Rottweiler.

It was getting dark as we pulled into the zoo parking lot, and as our car turned toward the zoo, we saw the security guard's truck. The headlights of our car swung toward his truck and we saw what he was observing. It was indeed a bear. It had four legs. Ladybug was on the loose outside the zoo in the park.

While Karen remained in the car with her headlights trained on the resting bear, I circled around and approached the bear cages. Pokey was in his cage watching his mate out in the park. Ladybug's cage had a large hole cut in the side. Vandals, it appeared, had been at work with some bolt cutters. Now, looking back on the incident, I imagine they were watching from the shadows with amusement.

Ladybug's escape pales in comparison to the one recorded by W. C. Coup in *Sawdust and Spangles*. Coup wrote about a polar bear that he imported to New York City in 1873 for his menagerie. He had sent an expedition to the Arctic and his men returned with two enormous bears. How they caught them, I can't imagine. They had no tranquilizer darts, and polar bears are much too smart to wander into a crude trap.

Lessons from the Zoo

In the process of transferring them from their shipping crates, one of the bears escaped and began a run down the middle of Fifth Avenue. Coup described the scene:

Children playing on the streets, seeing an immense white bear lumbering toward them at full speed, screamed and fled in every direction for shelter; horses, frightened at this unusual spectacle, became unmanageable and ran away; nurse-maids, wheeling their small charges, were stricken helpless with terror, and even the street dogs fled howling down the cross streets and into business houses. Everywhere disorder and terror reigned supreme; the streets became suddenly deserted, and one would have supposed that a plague had instantly depopulated the city. The police were called out from every adjacent station as soon as it became known that a white bear was loose in the streets of New York. The poor animal, unaccustomed to the strange medley of metropolitan civilization, was more frightened than those who fled before him. Finally, by the aid of the police and some of the braver citizens, the beast was driven into a basement of a private residence.

When I faced off with Ladybug, I was no stranger to working with bears. A dozen years earlier, when we were opening the Toronto Zoo, I worked extensively with polar bears. In fact, the first bears I ever worked with were two young polar bears that were being held in a facility known as the "Main Barn" across the street from the zoo. These two cubs were in adjacent pens with no shift doors. In order to clean their pens, we had to shift them out into a nearby hallway, utilizing plywood shields for protection. Although these animals were only a year old, they probably weighed over a hundred pounds each.

The procedure involved opening the gate to one of the animal's pens and entering with a shield and a broom to herd it out into the hallway. A second keeper, also armed with a broom and shield, guided the animal down the hall and into an empty cage. Once the cage was cleaned and fresh food and water supplied, the animal was herded back to where it began. The process was repeated for the second bear. It was exciting for us until they became large enough to snatch the shields out of our hands. We had some anxious moments until our overworked maintenance crew finally had the time to install some shift doors. Maybe that experience is what prepared me for my face-off with Ladybug a decade later.

As the grand opening of the Toronto Zoo drew near in August 1974, we had numerous bears arriving, departing, and needing care. At one point, I believe we had eight wild-caught polar bears in our collection. We had five youngsters, including Samantha, George, and Snowflake. We were in awe of Mr. Pooh, an enormous adult bear that had been trapped as a nuisance animal near Churchill, Manitoba. And we had two old bears named Amos and Andy that had lived across town at the Riverdale Zoo for more than twenty years.

Toronto's new polar bear habitat was a state-of-the-art facility with a large pool that featured underwater viewing. The barriers on the sides were tall, concrete walls while the back was intended to provide the illusion of open tundra into the distance. In order to allow that illusion, the designers included a deep, dry moat. The bears seemed to find this pit irresistible and they regularly fell into it. When we were not coaxing bears out of the moat, we were introducing them to each other. This was a significant challenge since polar bears are solitary animals by nature. We also dealt with abscessed canine teeth and infected sores between their toes.

Immobilizing polar bears could be tricky. The needles on the tranquilizer darts were exceptionally long, but their dense fur and thick layers of fat still interfered with a clean injection. Drugs that were meant to be injected into muscle frequently only made it into the fat. If the bear received a partial dose, giving a second injection risked a fatal overdose.

During these procedures, we waited until enough time had elapsed for the tranquilizer to take effect. If the animal appeared to be asleep, the veterinarian would carefully open the gate and push the bear with a broom handle. If the bear did not respond, we were in business. Often the bear would raise its head but be too groggy to bite at the stick. That was when the rodeo began. We would throw a towel over the bear's head and use the weight of a few hefty zookeepers to pin the animal to the floor. I spent many anxious moments in polar bear dens sprawled on top of groggy bears.

Some species of bears are highly adaptable. They are found in the Americas, Europe, and Asia and range in size from one-hundred-pound Sun bear of Southeast Asia and the Spectacled bear of South America to the massive, Northern latitude polar bears and brown bears that can weigh ten times that much. I grew up vacationing among the black bears of the Smokey Mountains. I have worked with grizzly bears, sloth bears, and polar bears. Few animals are less adaptable than polar bears.

I recall the transfer of six polar bears in Toronto, including Amos and Andy, to the new exhibit from the soon-to-be-closed Riverdale Zoo on October 17, 1974. Amos and Andy, as I recall, did not adapt well to their spacious new home. After being introduced to the new exhibit, they fell into the dry moat three times over their first few days. The change proved to be too much for them, and both were dead in less than a month.

When I worked at the Toledo Zoo in the 1990s, we undertook the construction of a new polar bear and seal exhibit we called the *Arctic Encounter*. As part of our design process, I was sent on a fact-finding mission to Churchill, Manitoba, on the Western shore of the Hudson Bay, just a few hundred miles south of the Arctic Circle. The population of Churchill was less than a thousand people and was located at the mouth of the Churchill River. In October, Churchill hosts dozens of wild polar bears as they wait for the ice shelf to form on Hudson Bay. That is why the town calls itself the Polar Bear Capital of the World.

My mission in July 1997 was to study polar bears and their habitat. After working with polar bears at the Toronto Zoo and receiving bears that had become a nuisance to populated cities and villages in their habitat, I was finally getting a look at the interactions firsthand.

We were informed that when the bears first became a problem in the 1960s, Canadian officials tried to relocate them. But the bears always returned. The solution was something called the polar bear jail. Nuisance bears were captured, held for a few months so they would forget where they were captured, and taken far from town for release.

As part of our fact-finding mission, we were treated to a helicopter tour. At one point, we landed and were allowed to crawl into an old bear den that had been dug into a bank next to a small pond. From the safety of the helicopter, we saw a female bear with two cubs, then another female, and later a large male. Within thirty miles of town, we saw a total of twelve bears, an Arctic fox, and hundreds of caribou.

The dominant trees in the area were the black spruce and the tamarack. We were at the northern edge of the tree line and most of the trees were stunted in size at four to six feet tall. They were estimated to be over a hundred years old. They should have looked like Christmas trees, and they were well-branched from the ground up to about six feet where the winter snow protected the foliage. But the branches above were scoured off the north side of the trees by the blowing winter snow, which we were told is so cold it is like ice pellets. The terrain, in addition to the evergreen trees on the high ground, was dominated by pothole ponds and low swampy areas.

I have had years of experience with captive polar bears. I have fed them, I have cleaned their dens, and I have been chased out of cages on several occasions during veterinary procedures when a bear woke up prematurely. Weighing in at a thousand pounds or more, their beady eyes are expressionless; they are utterly fearless and highly intelligent. I have seen a polar bear wiggle a paw under the caging into a hallway when people were present in a manner that indicated he could reach no farther. Anyone tempted to come toward the paw would have been in danger when they discovered he could grab them. They are wonderfully intelligent and charismatic creatures, but I have a hard time imagining a species that is less likely to adapt to being around humans. And with climate change melting the Arctic sea ice, it is not difficult to imagine polar bears becoming extinct in the wild. When people ask what is the most dangerous animal with which I have worked, my answer is always the polar bear. Fortunately for me, black bears are not as dangerous.

Ladybug was calm and did not appear inclined to wander too far from her cage, so I went to a storage shed and retrieved a catchpole and a plywood shield. My heart was racing as I positioned myself to drive her back to her cage. In all my years working with animals, this was the first time I had faced off with a large predator alone—and in the dark.

With the scene lit by the headlights of my wife's car and the guard's truck, I approached the bear and tapped the shield with the catchpole to get her attention. She turned to face me, pursed her lips, and gave a snort. I glanced at my car, gauging the distance in case I needed to scramble for cover. The lights were at my back, so the bear's view of me was probably not good. After a few moments, she turned and ambled toward her cage. I followed from a safe distance. Could it be this easy? Would she walk right back inside? Yep. I placed the plywood shield over the opening, secured it in place, and went home for the night.

It was standard procedure during my career that if an animal escaped, the first and best option was to offer it a way back to its cage. Animals are likely to prefer the safety of familiar territory. They have, in many cases, adapted to their homes at the zoo.

Some animals, like black bears, are extremely adaptable. They roam the mountains of Western North Carolina helping themselves to garbage, bird feeders, and whatever food they can find. People don't just tolerate them. They celebrate bear sightings. Polar bears, on the other hand, are dangerous predators. People are in peril when polar bears roam the streets of Churchill, Manitoba. That is why many of these pests end up being relocated to zoos. Now, as the planet warms, sea ice along the shores of Hudson Bay has become undependable. It forms later in the season and is less accommodating to the bears. If the bears cannot disperse and must remain in the town, both bears and humans will need to adapt.

Working with bears has taught me lesson seven, that we, as humans, must also adapt to change. And it may not just be the dynamic changes to our environment brought on by climate change that we will worry about. It may be that our ultimate challenges lie ahead as we figure out how to adapt to the aftermath of a global pandemic. Perhaps clues to successful adaptation will be found in the lives of some other animals—animals that inhabit our oceans.

LESSON 8

A Failure to Communicate

On a cool overcast afternoon in July 1997, I boarded a small boat with a half-dozen other people for a whale-watching cruise. This was not one of those large-scale ocean cruises, because these whales were spending the summer in an estuary at the mouth of Northern Canada's Churchill River where it flows into Hudson Bay. Since I was on a fact-finding trip as part of the planning process for the Toledo Zoo's polar bear exhibit, studying Beluga whales was not in our plans. This was just a bonus.

As our small boat motored away from the dock, I was skeptical about seeing whales. The water was calm, but the river was wide at this point and very murky. How we were to find whales, I had no idea, but as it turned out, we did not need to find them. They found us.

About twenty minutes into our cruise, they just appeared around the boat. There was no way to count them because they bobbed up to blow and breathe, then sank back down. I suppose there were ten or fifteen animals—many of them longer than our boat.

The beluga whale faces multiple threats from oil exploration and climate change, and it is still being captured for public display. It is an Arctic species that is relatively easy to capture because it is a slow swimmer that tends to gather in large numbers in estuaries and shallow coastal areas. Belugas have been hunted for centuries, and one of their earliest live-captures for an aquarium was documented by W. C. Coup.

In the spring of 1876, Coup formed a partnership with animal dealer Charles Reiche to start an enterprise that would come to be known as the New York Aquarium. The aquarium was built and opened later that year in the heart of Manhattan at Broadway and West Thirty-Fifth Street. Coup and Reiche were anxious to obtain "the largest living creatures of the deep." They launched an expedition to the Island of Coudres in Canada's St. Lawrence River to capture beluga whales. Coup provides a vivid account of their capture:

Lessons from the Zoo

Whales are timid, stupid creatures; in pursuit of small fish they run up close to the shore and are captured by a comparatively simple method. Across the mouth of some deep bay a line of piles is driven when the water is at low tide; then the fishing fleet only awaits the arrival of a school of Cetacea. These will sooner or later be seen rushing madly shoreward in pursuit of the schools of smaller fish on which they feed. When the whales are sighted the fishing vessels separate and endeavor to surround the assemblage of marine monsters. At high tide, when the line of piles is deeply submerged, the fleet crowds in toward the shore, and the frightened whales take refuge in the bay. Here they remain undisturbed and are generally quiet until they feel the tide receding. Then they become restless, and finally make a dash for deep water, only to run against the line of piles. It would be comparatively easy for a big whale to batter a great gap in the improvised fence, and, in fact, there is frequently room enough between certain piles for him to pass through unharmed, but he is naturally timid and cowardly, and when within a yard or two of the piles, wheels about and darts back in terror toward the shore. This fruitless and exhausting maneuver is kept up until the tide has completely gone out and he is left helpless and stranded. In all my experience in this peculiar line of live fishing I have never known a whale to break through the barrier of piles and make his escape.

J. D. Porter

The boxing and transportation to New York of these big fish was a great labor, and it often took fifty strong men several hours to get one of the monsters into its traveling case. Once in its box, water had to be poured over the back and blowholes of the imprisoned whale. The water pouring, by the way, was a monotonous and tiresome job which had to be continued without intermission during the subsequent ninety hours while the whale was being carried by vessel to Quebec, thence by rail via Montreal and Albany to New York. The water in which they lie must not cover their blow-holes, for, having no room to move they would be unable to rise and breathe and consequently would drown. Their boxes, therefore, were tight from the bottom up only as far as their eyes. Above that line there were cracks for the surplus water to flow off, and it was necessary for a man to stand over the whale and constantly drench him until the receiving tank was reached, a difficult undertaking.

Today, beluga whales are popular attractions at aquariums and marine parks throughout the world, but many of these facilities face a dilemma. Though belugas will breed and even rear their young in captivity, there are not nearly enough reaching adulthood to replenish captive populations. The United States and Canada do not allow the capture of belugas in their territorial waters. The only country that permits such captures is Russia. For North American facilities to import whales from Russia, they need a permit from the National Marine Fisheries Service, a part of the U.S. Department of Commerce's National Oceanic and Atmospheric Administration, and such permits are seldom issued.

The beluga whale (*Delphinapterus leucas*) is an Arctic and sub-Arctic cetacean. It has unique characteristics that are adapted to life in the Arctic. These include its all-white color and the absence of a dorsal fin, which allows belugas to swim under ice with ease. The beluga's body size is between that of a dolphin and a true whale, with males growing up to eighteen feet long and weighing over three thousand pounds. It is a stocky animal with a large percentage of its weight in fat.

Belugas are gregarious and form groups of ten animals on average, although during the summer, they can gather in the hundreds or even thousands in estuaries and shallow coastal areas. They are slow swimmers but can dive to a depth of over two-thousand feet. They are opportunistic feeders and their diets vary according to their locations and the season. Most belugas live in the Arctic Ocean and the seas and coasts around North America, Russia, and Greenland; their worldwide population is thought to number around 150,000. They are migratory and spend the winter around the Arctic ice cap. When the sea ice melts in summer, they move to warmer river estuaries and coastal areas.

The native peoples of North America and Russia have hunted belugas for centuries. They were also hunted by non-natives during the nineteenth century and part of the twentieth century. Hunting of belugas is not controlled by the International Whaling Commission, and each country has developed its own regulations.

Threats include natural predators like polar bears and orcas, contamination of rivers, and infectious diseases. The beluga was placed on the International Union for Conservation of Nature's Red List in 2008 as being "near threatened." Of seven Canadian beluga populations, those inhabiting eastern Hudson Bay (like the animals I observed), Ungava Bay, and the St. Lawrence River are listed as endangered.

They are cooperative animals and frequently hunt in coordinated groups. The animals in a pod are very sociable and will chase each other as if they are playing or fighting. They will even surface and dive together in a synchronized manner, in a behavior known as "milling".

In captivity, they are often seen playing vocalizing and swimming around each other. They show a curiosity towards humans and frequently approach the windows in the tanks to observe them. In 2009 during a free-diving competition in a tank of icy water in Harbin, China, a captive beluga reportedly brought a cramp-paralyzed diver from the bottom of the pool up to the surface by holding her foot in its mouth, saving the diver's life.

Lessons from the Zoo

The very next year, in contrast, a trainer at SeaWorld in Florida was dragged into the water, battered, and drowned by a different kind of "whale." The killer whale or orca (*Orcinus orca*) is not a true whale. It is the largest member of the dolphin family. Though orcas and belugas are large, social, ocean dwellers, the contrast between these species is great. Belugas subsist on a diet of fish, octopus, and squid. Orcas patrol the world's oceans, hunting in packs and preying on everything from fish to seals. They have even been known to attack belugas. But there is a similarity in the way they communicate since both species depend heavily on underwater sound for orientation, feeding, and communication. Orcas produce clicks, whistles, and pulsed calls that are even broken down into unique dialects for individual pods.

The belugas I saw in Canada seemed curious as they swam alongside our boat. I later learned that they also play with objects they find in the water; in the wild, they do this with wood, plants, dead fish, and bubbles they have created. During the breeding season, adults have been observed carrying objects such as plants, nets, and even the skeleton of a dead reindeer on their heads and backs. Captive females have also been observed displaying this behavior, carrying items such as floats and buoys, after they have lost a calf. Experts consider this interaction with the objects to be a substitute behavior.

Belugas use echolocation for movement, to find breathing holes in the ice, and to hunt in dark or turbid waters. A protuberance at the front of its head houses a large, flexible echolocation organ called the melon. They produce a rapid sequence of clicks that pass through the melon, which acts as an acoustic lens to focus the sounds into a beam that is projected forward through the surrounding water. These sounds spread through the water at a speed of nearly two kilometers per second, some four times faster than the speed of sound in air. The sound waves reflect from objects and return as echoes that are heard and interpreted by the animal. This enables them to determine the distance, speed, size, shape, and the object's internal structure within the beam of sound. In addition to the clicks they use for navigation, these animals communicate using sounds of high-frequency whistles. Their calls can sound like bird songs, earning them the nickname "canaries of the sea." Like the other toothed whales, belugas do not possess vocal cords and the sounds are probably produced by the movement of air between the nasal sacks, which are located near to the blowhole.

There is heavy debate as to whether cetacean vocalizations can constitute a language. A study conducted in 2015 determined that European beluga signals share physical features comparable to "vowels." These sounds were found to be stable throughout time but varied among different geographical locations. The further away the populations were from each other, the more varied the sounds were in relation to one another.

I have never worked with belugas in captivity, but my brief experience with them in the wild changed the way I see aquatic mammals. When the guide on our 1997 Churchill River excursion lowered a microphone, called a hydrophone, into the water, we heard the high-pitched chirps, squeaks, and squeals of wild beluga whales coming from the small boom box at the back of the boat. It was the chatter of a whale family on an outing, talking to each other as they made their way up the river. They seemed unconcerned over our presence—innocent and vulnerable.

Hearing the belugas reminded me of Carl Sagan's 1985 science fiction novel, *Contact*. It deals with the exciting prospect of human contact with intelligent, extraterrestrial life. It seems to me that we have intelligent, extraterrestrial life forms in our oceans. I have heard them and wonder what I would say to them if I could talk back. My first words would probably be an apology for how humans have treated them.

Consider this quote by Henry Beston, who said in his 1928 book, *The Outermost House: A Year of Life on the Great Beach of Cape Cod*:

We patronize [animals] for their incompleteness, for their tragic fate for having taken form so far be-

low ourselves. And therein do we err. For the animal shall not be measured by man. In a world older and more complete than ours, they move finished and complete, gifted with the extension of the senses we have lost or never attained, living by voices we shall never hear. They are not brethren, they are not underlings: they are other nations, caught with ourselves in the net of life and time, fellow prisoners of the splendor and travail of the earth.

Lesson eight—the importance of communication—has long been a challenge for me because I have never been a good communicator. I once had a counselor tell me that, in order to save my marriage, I needed to open up and let my wife know what I was thinking. In my career, I have been better at "communicating" with the animals. I have crooned soothing words to an elephant in order to bring him back in line as I heard the rumbling that may indicate his infrasonic communication. I have allowed a disoriented baby gorilla to sit in my lap—until he bit me. And I have willed an escaped black bear to go back into her cage.

I had a friend in college who was blind but used the tap of his cane to navigate around campus by echolocation. Richard Louv, in his latest book, *Our Wild Calling*, suggests that humans may be able to communicate with more than just the five senses of taste, touch, smell, sight, and hearing. Some scientists suggest we may be able to utilize something bordering on telepathy—some type of natural brain to brain Wi-Fi.

Then there is the story of a guy who posted a sign outside his house that said, "Talking dog for sale." The sign intrigued a passerby who knocked on the door and went inside to talk to the dog.

"So," the visitor began, "what have you done with your life?"

"I've led a full life," said the dog. "I lived for a while in the Alps, where I rescued avalanche victims. I served my country during two tours of Iraq. And now I spend my days reading to residents in a retirement home."

The visitor was flabbergasted and asked the owner, "Why on earth would you want to get rid of an incredible dog like this?"

"Because," said the owner, "that dog is a liar. He never did any of that stuff."

We clearly have much to learn about communication. One way I have attempted to improve my own communication skill is to listen more closely to the chirps, caws, and melodies of the birds in my own backyard.

LESSON 9

An Appreciation of Nature

On my first trip to Africa in March 1986, the first animals I noted in my journal were not giraffes or lions. They were birds. We began seeing them as soon as we landed, and I noted in my journal that "the variety was astonishing." Just outside our room at the Boulevard Hotel in downtown Nairobi, my wife and I spotted a pair of Hadada ibis poking their long beaks into the stream bank. Raucous black and white pied crows hopped around in the trees, disturbing the weaver birds who tended their pendulous, basket-like nests. Stunning carmine-red bee-eaters flitted above the stream picking off insects on the wing, and my wife noted that the metallic blue, green, and red superb starlings really were "superb."

Later, as we drove around the countryside, we were excited to see black kites soaring high above the ostrich and secretary birds that patrolled the fields beside the road. We marveled at the oxpeckers who clung to the backs of Cape buffalo like feathery gymnasts and the cattle egrets who followed the buffalo herd, snapping up the bugs they disturbed.

Every lodge seemed to have its resident population of marabou storks hanging around the garbage dump. We sat around the pool at Lake Nakuru Lodge, about a hundred miles north of Nairobi, watching them fly in. They looked like airliners on approach until they put down their landing gear and we saw two, long stick-like appendages dangling beneath their bulky bodies. We waited for them to stumble, but they never did.

My wife and I have long been bird watchers. We enjoy observing them, identifying them, and attracting them to our back yard. When we lived in Tampa, we were awakened every morning, not by a rooster crowing, but a raucous blue jay perched outside our bedroom window.

I did grow up hearing roosters crowing in the morning. My dad kept chickens. We gathered eggs, and he wrung their necks when it was time to eat them. I'm sure we had plenty of wild birds around our house but the only ones I distinctly remember were the coveys of quail that scampered into our yard at the edge of the woods. As an adult, my wife and I enjoyed the birds in our yards when we lived in Sioux Falls, Toledo, and Albany, Georgia.

We especially enjoy the exotic birds when we travel. Our bookshelves at home include volumes on the birds of Belize, Costa Rica, Canada, East Africa, Britain, and Europe. After our trip to Belize, she documented our experience by doing a large painting that hangs in our bedroom. It represents a lush landscape with a Mayan ruin in the distance. But the painting features birds—collared aracari, blue-crowned motmot, violaceous trogon, great kiskadee, and ferruginous pygmy owl.

I have searched for the elusive resplendent quetzal in the cloud forests of Costa Rica, marveled at the primitive hoatzin in a tributary of the Amazon river deep in the jungles of Ecuador, and gingerly stepped over nesting blue-footed boobies in the Galapagos Islands.

I have worked with and cared for birds in zoos—from the wattled cranes, Stanley cranes, marabou storks, and ostrich at Busch Gardens in the 1970s to the group of flamingos we imported for a new display in Albany, Georgia, in 2006. I oversaw the construction of the aviary at the Lowry Park Zoo in the 1980s and the award-winning renovation of the Bird House at the Toledo Zoo in the 1990s.

What is it about birds? They fly in and out of our lives like fleeting memories. They represent the natural world as they inspire an appreciation for nature and remind me of its importance in my life. They also played a unique role in my retirement—a role that might seem incongruous to some.

I am not a hunter. It's not that I disapprove, it's just that shooting guns and killing animals is not my thing. I have, however, seen lions in Africa kill an antelope. It is a different experience in person than it is on television. It is more visceral, more intense, and it helped me realize that it is perfectly natural for one animal to die in order to feed another.

I grew up on the Gulf Coast of Florida where my dad not only killed chickens for food, he taught me and my brothers to catch fish and gather oysters and scallops from the Gulf of Mexico in order to feed our family. We were poor, and in a rural culture, hunting and fishing are a way of life. Hunting puts meat from deer, turkeys, ducks, and quail in the freezer and is passed down through the generations. That's why, after retiring from a forty-year career working with animals in zoos, I felt comfortable accepting a part-time job driving a mule wagon at a local quail hunting lodge. The lure of being in nature and working with mules and dogs was too much to resist. It afforded me a marvelous platform from which to observe the natural world, which, in my case, was the longleaf pine savanna—an ecosystem that is sustained by fire.

It was not at all unusual for the guests on my wagon to observe, "It looks like you've had a fire come through here."

Lessons from the Zoo

They were noticing the blackened trunks of all the mature pine trees that dot the landscape.

"We burn this property every year," I would reply, much to their surprise.

This is where I gave a brief summary of a complicated concept. Without the regular destruction by fire, this ideal bobwhite quail habitat would not exist. Fire is a natural phenomenon that some ecosystems require. If we suppress it, those ecosystems will cease to exist.

Pine trees have evolved to withstand fire. Everything else pretty much burns to the ground. But within days, a miracle happens. Shoots of green begin to appear from the blackened soil. In a few weeks, the ground is a carpet of greenery and in a few months, evidence of the fire has been replaced by lush, wildlife-supporting vegetation.

I often wondered, as I sat on my wagon and watched the hunters stalk the broomsedge and wiregrass hoping to flush another covey, what that landscape would look like without quail hunters paying for its preservation. My guess is that the wide-open, pine-wiregrass habitat would be swallowed up in a scrub oak forest. The quail, gopher tortoise, and other savanna-loving creatures would disappear.

The longleaf pine savanna—the signature ecosystem of the American Southeast—is said to have once covered more than 50 percent of the land across thousands of miles of nine states, from Virginia to East Texas. In the *Sierra Club Magazine*, the famed biologist E. O. Wilson wrote an essay titled, *It's Time to Strike a Fair Deal with Wild Nature* (January 2016). In it, he identified twelve of the "best places in the biosphere"—places like the Amazon River basin and the Serengeti grasslands. These places, Wilson suggested, are some of the best places to see a living natural environment. Wilson listed the longleaf pine savanna of the American Southeast as one of the twelve. It is, I believe, quail hunting that has preserved enough habitat to make this list.

For those who seriously and actively care about animals, there are, I believe, several types of animal lovers. They include animal activists, animal care professionals, and sportsmen. It is the sportsmen—hunters and fishermen—who are usually left out of the conversation when it comes to a love of animals because they express their respect by harvesting and consuming the very things they love and seek to protect.

Much of society, it seems, is disconnected from the source of our food. Deep down, we know that if we eat meat, some animal had to provide that meat; but it is not something to be talked about in polite society.

This was illustrated a few years ago when my wife, an elementary school librarian, was speaking to a first-grade class. She had just read them a story about what animals eat and explained the differences between carnivores, herbivores, and omnivores. But when my wife asked the kids what category humans fall into, the children became confused. Many did not realize that humans eat other animals—that when eating hamburger, they are eating a cow or when consuming bacon, they are eating a pig. This urban generation is being raised on shrink-wrapped food from the grocery store. I wondered if some parents might be upset that their children were being told otherwise.

Why the disconnect? Perhaps it is because we don't want to think about the fact that animals are killed to supply our meat. We are content with an illusion.

This illusion reminds me of the story (probably untrue, but a good story nonetheless) about a display presented by showman P. T. Barnum early in his career. It was called *The Happy Family*, and it is said to have featured a lion, a tiger, a panther, and a lamb—all in the same cage. After the exhibition had been running for a while, a friend asked the showman how everything was going. "Oh, fairly well," Barnum replied. "I'm going to make a permanent feature out of it, if the supply of lambs holds out."

The guests I met on my wagon were, for the most part, enthusiastic sportsmen. They loved shooting the way some people love golf, even to the point of cheering the well-placed shot. Most of them were more like me than I ever suspected. They were naturalists at heart. They may have flown in on private jets and carried shotguns that cost more than a new car, but they still marveled at the vultures that soared overhead, asked about the prescribed fire that maintains quail habitat, and got excited when a Cooper's hawk swooped in to seize a quail in mid-flight.

They were as knowledgeable about what quail eat as they were what size shotgun shell would bring them down, and they believed in giving the birds a sporting chance to get away. Most would not shoot unless their target was well into the air and flapping madly in the opposite direction.

Author Temple Grandin uses her autism and her expertise as an animal science professor at Colorado State University as a platform to advocate for the humane treatment of the livestock we slaughter for food. In her 2009 book, *Animals Make Us Human*, she suggests that our relationship with the animals we use for food should be mutually beneficial. If we are going to take animals for food, then we should provide those animals a good quality of life before that use.

The birds that were killed in our operation were dropped in a box on the wagon and placed on ice after each hunt. They were then cleaned, packaged, and frozen—ready for consumption by our guests. They were harvested at least as humanely as the billions of chickens who are slaughtered every year to provide our chicken nuggets and many more quail escape than are shot. I know because I saw them fly into the distance and later heard them mock us with their calls as we drove in at the end of the day.

Hunters raise millions of dollars every year for wildlife conservation and habitat preservation. They do it by directly supporting the operations where they hunt and through organizations like Quail Unlimited and Ducks Unlimited. And they do it through state game license fees. According to recent media reports, the decline in the number of hunters has caused a significant reduction in the collection of these fees and is threatening how we pay for conservation. Perhaps the people who oppose hunting as cruel and barbaric might see the end of hunting as a victory, but from where I sat on the wagon, it would be a hollow victory indeed.

My own affinity for the land began as a boy growing up in Florida, dodging rattlesnakes as I wandered among the palmettos and pine trees in the woods behind my house. My adult adventures have seen me slogging through northern hardwood forests in knee-deep snow and sleeping in a tent on the Serengeti grasslands where hippos brushed the side of my tent at night. I have been blessed to observe thousands of wildebeest crossing a river in Africa, to swim with fur seals in the Galapagos Islands, and to hear the calls of beluga whales in the Arctic.

In his 2005 book *Last Child in the Woods*, author Richard Louv coined the term "Nature-Deficit Disorder" to link the lack of nature in the lives of today's wired generation to some of the most disturbing childhood trends, such as rises in obesity,

Attention Deficit Disorder (ADD), and depression. He claims that by the 1990s, the radius around the home where children could roam on their own had shrunk to one-ninth of what it had been in 1970. Today, Louv says, average eight-year-olds are better able to identify cartoon characters than native species, such as beetles and oak trees, in their own community.

There is, I believe, no substitute for being in nature and no reason we can't find nature even in the most urban environments. Whether it is in a park, a hunting lodge, or our own backyard, nature is in our genes, and we need nature as much as it needs us to save it.

During our trip to Africa in the 1980s, I saw flamingos lining the shores of Lake Nakuru in numbers that were too large to count. It looked like millions to me. The pink ribbon of birds that edged the shore of the massive lake reminded me of a work of art that was on display at the time in Miami, Florida. A Bulgarian artist known as Christo and his crew had laboriously unfurled millions of square feet of specially made pink fabric for seven miles up and down the Biscayne Bay in 1983 to make something he called Art Islands.

Seeing the flamingos in mass along the shore like a Christo Art Island was like life imitating art. But even more remarkable for me was seeing the flamingos in flight after a career of managing non-flying birds in zoos. Of all the animals I saw in Africa, from lions and elephants to wildebeest and crocodiles, seeing the birds at Lake Nakuru was one of the few times I noted a "moving experience" in my journal.

It took me a lifetime of travel and observation around the world to appreciate the fact that the birds that fly in and out of my backyard are as wild and exotic at the flamingos at Lake Nakuru. It also took me a lifetime of fresh starts and uncertain futures to know that birds anchor me to a spot in the world. They bring me joy, whether it is seeing the resplendent quetzal in the cloud forests of Costa Rica life or a hummingbird at the feeder in my backyard. Birds represent the freedom we all yearn for, and they inspire lesson nine. We need to take more time to appreciate nature.

LESSON 10

Seize the Day

To say I love dogs would be an understatement. Dogs have been a part of my life since the day I was born. My childhood dogs were yard dogs that never came in the house, but in those days, children seldom went in the house either, except to eat or sleep. Dogs ran with us, or we ran with them.

I grew up with Mitsy, Tippy, and Snoopy—yard dogs that ran through the woods around our house. They seldom if ever went to a vet, and when it was their time, they simply went off into the woods to die. We always wondered if they met up with the rattlesnakes we were warned about. Looking back, I wonder they were better or worse off than the pampered dogs that lived inside my house and died of age-related illnesses like cancer. In my adult life, my wife and I have always had one or two dogs as part of the family, and I still grieve for those that have passed. We shared our home and our lives with Simba and Jana for fourteen years, then Chelsea and Bexley for another twelve years.

Maybe that is why I had such an affinity for the dogs in the hunting operation that occupied the early years of my retirement and why I loved spending time with a dog named Joy on my lap.

A quail hunt, at least on the property where I worked, was filled with pageantry. We arrived under the ancient live oaks surrounding the "big house" at nine o'clock in the morning—two mule-drawn wagons with six or eight horses led by hunting guides in white vests. It was such an impressive sight that first-time guests often stood on the porch and took video of the procession with their cell phones.

In all this pageantry—mules, horses, wagons, and guides—one individual was often singled out. She stood on the seat of the first wagon, as she had done for nearly a decade, and was clearly the star of the show. She was a thirty-pound chocolate brown English cocker named Joy.

Dogs are an essential part of a quail hunt. Every morning, after we loaded guests and guns and rode out to the hunting grounds, the first order of business was to stop and get two dogs out of the wagon. They were English pointers, muscular little shorthaired dogs with names like Buck and Gabby, Bud and Pearl, and Ike and Dot.

Lessons from the Zoo

They were taken out of the wagon in a male-female pair and positioned side by side in the middle of the road, with a gentle tug on their collars and an equally gentle command to "whoa." The dog handler's control was impressive and was probably the result of hours, weeks, and, even, years of training. The dogs stood still and looked at their handler as he mounted his horse. They were listening for their release—a low whistle, not unlike the whistle of the bobwhite quail.

Once released, they ran up and down the dirt roads and in and out of the grassy lanes. By all outward appearances, they were running aimlessly at a brisk lope—aimlessly, that is, until one of them caught the scent of quail in the thick grass. Then it looked like the dog had come to the end of some invisible leash. His head snapped toward the birds and his body jerked sideways. He remained immobile with head down and tail up. The other dog was usually not nearby, but when she saw her partner's point, she stopped and fell into a less serious point, essentially honoring her partner.

Our guide would turn back to the wagon and say, "We've got a point up here."

It's still a bit of a mystery to me, especially from my vantage point on the wagon, how the dog handler interpreted the actions of the dogs. He seemed to know whether the dog was pointing at a covey, a single bird, or a dead bird that had been the morning meal for a hawk. Were both dogs on the same covey, or were there, in fact, two coveys? This was the heart of the hunt—the dogs on point and the guide positioning the hunters, followed by the moment of truth when the birds flew, the guns boomed, and the birds fell. This was when Joy, the little English cocker on the wagon seat next to me, stopped whining and jumping around. She stood at full alert and went silent as she awaited the dog handler's call.

Most of the birds fell in an open area where they were easily picked up. Occasionally, however, a bird fell into the deep grass. That took a little more looking, even when the hunter knew where the bird fell. After a few moments of fruitless searching, the call went up from the guide as he looked back to the wagon and yelled, "JOY!"

Joy scrambled down the steps at the side of the wagon and navigated the lanes to where the hunters and guides waited. The guide pointed and said, "bird in here," and Joy went to work. She scrambled back and forth, nose to the ground in ever-shrinking circles until she homed in on her target. Finally, she dove in with nose down, butt in the air, and tail constantly wagging and emerged with a bird in her mouth. She looked to the guide who said "wagon" and back she came to deliver the bird to me and turn her attention back to the action in the field.

This was clearly a highlight for the hunters and was the reason that after nearly a dozen seasons, Joy was the star of the show. She was the enthusiastic magician pulling an invisible bird out of the deep grass and bounding back to the wagon with her treasure. That is, I suppose, why Joy was the first one the hunters greet when they come out on the porch of the house in the morning and the last one to be touched with an affectionate pat on the head before they headed in for drinks after the hunt. Who could blame her for reveling in her position as the center of attention, and who could blame her for resenting it when a series of young cockers joined our wagon?

At thirteen years of age, Joy had not simply lost a step or two. On some hot days, she returned to the wagon, too exhausted to climb the steps. She had to stop and catch her breath before clambering up to deliver her bird and flop down on the seat beside me. That was why the young dogs began riding the wagon—to take some of the pressure off Joy. She didn't appear to appreciate their assistance. She snapped at them when they hopped around on the wagon, and she watched their every move from the wagon seat when they were called down to find a bird.

As a retiree myself, I always enjoyed it when the youngsters had a hard time finding a bird and Joy had to be called down to show them how it was done.

I recently learned that we share our world with about a billion dogs. We have around seventy-five million in the United States, alone. Dogs evolved from an ancestor of the gray wolf, which has been around for three-hundred thousand years. But how did we get to the modern dog from this ruthless carnivore and apex predator with its bone-splintering bite?

The earliest dogs appeared about fifteen thousand years ago when humans began displacing Neanderthals in Northern Europe and Asia. But the explosion of diversity in shape and size only occurred about two hundred years ago with a breeding craze in Europe and the advent of kennel clubs in the 1800s. Dogs are great companions and have been bred to hunt, herd, and protect. But they can also learn an astonishing variety of tasks. They assist us in therapy, search and rescue, policing, and even in war.

Most surprising to me is the recent speculation that humans did not domesticate wolves. Wolves domesticated themselves. They accomplished this by staying in proximity to human settlements, scavenging our leftovers, and adapting to our ways over generations. Wolves evolved into dogs and became hunting companions that were a perfect complement to humans. Dogs were the chasers, and humans were the finishers. We both shared in the spoils of the hunt.

In the 1989 film *Dead Poets Society*, actor Robin Williams sensationalized the Latin phrase, *carpe diem*. It is taken from the Roman poet, Horace, who said in about 65 BCE, "Seize the day; put no trust in the morrow."

But even Horace was not the first philosopher to recognize the importance of living in the present. Lao Tzu who lived in China nearly five hundred years before Horace said, "If you are depressed, you are living in the past. If you are anxious, you are living in the future. If you are at peace, you are living in the present."

I have always thought the story of Adam and Eve eating the forbidden fruit was a metaphor for what makes us distinct from the animals. In the middle of God's garden were two trees, the tree of life and the tree of the knowledge of good and evil. God commanded Adam not to eat from the tree of the knowledge of good and evil, suggesting that if he did, he "will surely die." When Adam and Eve did eat of that tree, they separated themselves from the animal kingdom. They knew what it was to be naked and afraid (hmm—sounds like the title of a television show). That is, I suppose, when we humans began to worry.

I am a world-class worrier. I don't dwell on the past too much, and I am largely content with the present, but when it comes to the future, I worry. I just can't help myself. Maybe that's why I have such an affinity for dogs. They don't worry about the future. Dogs don't do "what if?" In fact, I should heed this advice I recently saw on a sign somewhere for how a dog handles worry: *If you can't eat it, play with it, then pee on it and walk away.*

When I was driving the wagon, I spent most afternoons with my feet propped up, my hands firmly on the reins, and Joy standing in my lap. I watched vultures floating in a cloudless sky, felt the breeze as it rustled the pine trees before me, and listened for the call of bobwhite quail in the sea of tall grass.

Joy, like most dogs, had a way of squeezing the most out of every moment. When the hunters were stalking and shooting, she whined and moved around in anticipation of being called down to find birds. But when the shooting stopped and the guides and hunters were picking up their harvest, she stood still, barely breathing in anticipation of hearing her name called to find a bird. This cycle repeated until the end of the hunt, and we were riding in to drop off the guests. That is when she laid down on the seat next to me fully relaxed.

That, I suppose, is why I have such an affinity for dogs. I envy them. With a dog, there is no discussion of how the day went; no complaining about the weather; and no worries about what's for dinner. With a dog, there is just the contentment of the moment. While most animals retain some of their wildness, dogs gave that up to live and work with us.

A final word about living in the present moment comes from another Latin phrase. *Memento Mori* means "remember you must die." Its origins go all the way back to Plato, and it is not used in a morbid sense. *Memento mori* is meant to remind us of the transient nature of life and that we need to live in the present moment.

At the end of the day, Joy did not appear to be worried about going back to the kennel. She didn't seem to dread spending another night alone. She didn't wish the wagon would slow down or speed up. Joy was lost in the moment and doing what I wish I could learn to do more of, appreciate life.

The final lesson—Lesson Ten—is *carpe diem*.

BONUS LESSON

Love Your Neighbor

Dogs are the animals that bookend my life's story. They protected me when I was a child. They shared my home and marriage, helped me raise children, and comforted me in retirement. But I hesitate to say dogs are my outright favorite because so many animals—from elephants to apes—have touched my life. In many ways, the animals in this book are as much a part of my life story as my wife, my children, and my grandchildren.

When I retired in 2015 and found myself driving a mule wagon, the long periods of quiet as I sat on that wagon reminded me of the quote often attributed to Winnie the Pooh author, A. A. Milne: *Sometimes I sits and thinks, and sometimes I just sits.* But even when I was "just sitting," I was aware of how much I loved the animals that surrounded me—not only the mules, the horses, and the dogs but also the quail hiding in the tall grass and the hawks waiting in nearby trees for a chance to eat them. My connection was direct, powerful, and undeniable. It caused me to reflect on that June 1972 article which featured me as a fresh-faced zookeeper. The writer said I was a sensitive young man whose life revolved around a love of animals. He noted a spiritual dimension to zoos and suggested I was maintaining contact with mankind's biological heritage. I was, he said, experiencing the power of wildness in an almost mystical way.

I have a degree in Zoology and have studied animals and natural history for many years, so I consider myself a scientist. But as I think about my "mystical connection" to nature and how it played out in my connection to the animals I cared for over the past fifty years, I come down to how my belief in God has shaped that connection.

Discussing religion in a book based on animal science is a bit like passing gas in the first-class section of a crowded airplane. It is sure to elicit more than a few dirty looks and mumbled comments. Religion, after all, is about humans and how we alone were made in the image of God. Religion has been used as the justification for humans to do just about anything we want—including making war on each other. But if we can step away from religion and focus instead on spirituality, perhaps a connection will become evident.

Even scientists must admit to having faith in things unseen. Look at their search for something called the God Particle. The Higgs boson is the smallest elementary particle in physics. Despite supposedly being present everywhere, the existence of the Higgs field has been extremely hard to confirm. The search for this elusive particle has taken more than forty years and led to the construction of one of the world's most expensive and complex experimental facilities to date, the Hadron Collider near Geneva, Switzerland. It is dedicated to the pursuit of the fundamental science of something scientists have fully embraced but do not fully understand.

Dark Matter or Dark Energy is another concept about which more is still unknown than is known. Scientists can calculate a quantity of dark matter because they know how it affects the universe's expansion. They tell us that while 5 percent of the universe is made up of "regular" matter that we can see and feel, the other 95 percent is a complete mystery.

And then there is a little thing called the Big Bang. The very origin of our universe is explained through models and mathematical formulas, but I am not sure anyone really knows how it all began or what was there before the Big Bang. Science, it would seem, also relies on "faith in things unseen."

Perhaps the fundamental division between science and spirituality is the definition of "God." I was raised a Christian and make no apology for finding strength and comfort in the teachings of Jesus—not the man on whom we base a religion, but the man who taught us that God was to be found in how we love one another. But when I saw the Star Wars films, I was struck by the similarities between my understanding of God and what the films called "the Force." It made me wonder about the gods that are worshiped by Muslims, Jews, and countless other religions around the world.

The ancients are said to have divided humans into three parts. One part of us is the physical body—our flesh and blood. A second part might be called the soul. That is that physical part of us—that something called "life"—that we share with all animals. And finally, we have a spirit—our kinship to God that makes us a rational creature. It is something we consider to be unique to mankind. But I wonder if that is true. I suspect that, one day, we will discover that even our spirit is not unique to humans. Perhaps the spirit of God is more akin to the Force in Star Wars than to an old man with a white beard who lives in a place called Heaven. The god that I can best relate to is omnipotent and genderless and encompasses all living creatures. A God that can explain the unknown like the Big Bang, how monarch butterflies find their way to Mexico every year, and what those beluga whales were saying to each other as they swam alongside my boat in the Churchill River.

Jane Goodall has suggested in her writing that there is an element of pure spirit that is in each of us. She suggests that if we can learn to understand that spirit, perhaps we can reach out beyond "the narrow prison of our own lives" and begin to understand the supernatural power that we call "God, or Allah, the Tao, Brahma, the Creator, or whatever our personal belief prescribes." If we can figure out how to do that, perhaps we could create a better world.

Humans have embraced a concept of god and some type of creation story for all recorded history. Perhaps this was the first stage of our evolution that we began to recognize that we were "special" and that all humans have some spark of the divine.

But that divine spark has caused us to be separate and alone as a species. The world is a multi-species community that humans place ourselves above and refuse to join. I wonder if the next stage of our evolution is when we recognize our divine relationship with all living things, including our planet. What will it take for us to give up our exalted position as rulers of the earth and recognize that we must become part of the earth in partnership with plants and animals? Maybe it will take COVID-19 or the next viral pandemic to get our attention.

When Jesus was asked what he considered the greatest commandment that stood above all other teachings, he replied:

Love the Lord your God with all your heart and with all your soul and with all your mind. This is the first and greatest commandment. And the second is like it: Love your neighbor as yourself. All the Law and the Prophets hang on these two commandments.

Matthew 22:36-40

Jesus does not define "neighbor," and it would presumptuous to extend its meaning–but I am going to, anyway. Not all our neighbors are human. Perhaps this is where science and spirituality (and even religion) can come together and perhaps **love your neighbor** is the final and most important lesson of all.

ABOUT THE AUTHOR

J. D. (Doug) Porter is a retired zoologist and author who has a bachelor's degree in zoology and a master's in adult education. Doug blogs on a range of subjects related to animals, nature, and the environment. He has written two novels, *The Menagerie: A Zoo Story* and *The Dogcatcher and The Fox*.

Lessons from the Zoo is his memoir.

www.ingramcontent.com/pod-product-compliance
Lightning Source LLC
Chambersburg PA
CBHW071348080526
44587CB00017B/3017